Casseroles
& One-Dish Meals
VOLUME 2

RDA ENTHUSIAST BRANDS, LLC
MILWAUKEE, WI

Taste of Home

Reader's digest

A TASTE OF HOME/READER'S DIGEST BOOK

© 2015 RDA Enthusiast Brands, LLC, 1610 N. 2nd St., Suite 102, Milwaukee WI 53212. All rights reserved.
Taste of Home and Reader's Digest are registered trademarks of The Reader's Digest Association, Inc.

EDITORIAL
Editor-in-Chief: Catherine Cassidy
Creative Director: Howard Greenberg
Editorial Operations Director: Kerri Balliet

Managing Editor, Print & Digital Books: Mark Hagen
Associate Creative Director: Edwin Robles Jr.

Editors: Michelle Rozumalski, Amy Glander
Layout Designer: Courtney Lovetere
Editorial Production Manager: Dena Ahlers
Copy Chief: Deb Warlaumont Mulvey
Copy Editors: Joanne Weintraub, Dulcie Shoener
Contributing Copy Editor: Steph Kilen
Content Operations Assistant: Shannon Stroud
Editorial Services Administrator: Marie Brannon

Food Editors: James Schend; Peggy Woodward, RD
Recipe Editors: Mary King; Jenni Sharp, RD; Irene Yeh

Test Kitchen & Food Styling Manager: Sarah Thompson
Test Cooks: Nicholas Iverson (lead), Matthew Hass,
Lauren Knoelke
Food Stylists: Kathryn Conrad (lead), Leah Rekau,
Shannon Roum
Prep Cooks: Megumi Garcia, Melissa Hansen,
Bethany Van Jacobson, Sara Wirtz

Photography Director: Stephanie Marchese
Photographers: Dan Roberts, Jim Wieland
Photographer/Set Stylist: Grace Natoli Sheldon
Set Stylists: Stacey Genaw, Melissa Haberman,
Dee Dee Jacq
Photo Studio Assistant: Ester Robards

Editorial Business Manager: Kristy Martin
Editorial Business Associate: Samantha Lea Stoeger

BUSINESS
Vice President, Group Publisher: Kirsten Marchioli
Publisher: Donna Lindskog
General Manager, Taste of Home Cooking School:
Erin Puariea
Executive Producer, Taste of Home Online Cooking School:
Karen Berner

THE READER'S DIGEST ASSOCIATION, INC.
President and Chief Executive Officer: Bonnie Kintzer
Vice President, Chief Operating Officer, North America:
Howard Halligan
Chief Revenue Officer: Richard Sutton
Chief Marketing Officer: Leslie Dukker Doty
Vice President, Content Marketing & Operations:
Diane Dragan
Senior Vice President, Global HR & Communications:
Phyllis E. Gebhardt, SPHR
Vice President, Brand Marketing: Beth Gorry
Vice President, Chief Technology Officer: Aneel Tejwaney
Vice President, Consumer Marketing Planning: Jim Woods

For other Taste of Home books and products,
visit us at **tasteofhome.com.**

For more Reader's Digest products and information, visit
rd.com (in the United States) or **rd.ca** (in Canada).

International Standard Book Number: 978-1-61765-457-2
Library of Congress Control Number: 2015937793

Cover Photographer: Grace Natoli Sheldon
Set Stylist: Melissa Haberman
Food Stylist: Shannon Roum

Pictured on front cover:
Ravioli Lasagna, page 66

Pictured on back cover: Chicken Cheese Strata, page 192;
Berry-Topped Puff Pancake, page 28

EZ-READ is a trademark of RDA Enthusiast Brands, LLC.

Printed in China.
3 5 7 9 10 8 6 4 2

FRITO PIE, 184

EASY CHEDDAR CHICKEN POTPIE, 100

CRANBERRY CORN BREAD CASSEROLE, 47

CORNED BEEF HASH AND EGGS, 19

CONTENTS

 LIKE US
facebook.com/tasteofhome

 TWEET US
@tasteofhome

 FOLLOW US
pinterest.com/taste_of_home

SHOP WITH US
shoptasteofhome.com

SHARE A RECIPE
tasteofhome.com/submit

MIDWEST MEATBALL
CASSEROLE, 62

Share a **Satisfying Favorite** Tonight!

Today's home cooks know how to dish out the comforting goodness that can only be found in a heartwarming casserole... and they're sharing their secrets with you in this collection, **Taste of Home Casseroles & One-Dish Meals!**

These are the tried-and-true casseroles **family cooks** turn to time and again. Now you can dig into any of these **112 recipes** for a meal-in-one that's sure to satisfy.

From **overnight breakfast bakes** to **cheesy dinner entrees**, the dishes in this **easy-to-read** cookbook are sure to become new staples in your home.

FARMER'S STRATA, 20

Look for these handy icons for quick meal planning:

FREEZE IT

Store these casseroles in the freezer for busy nights.

POTLUCK

Need a dish to pass? Turn to these crowd-pleasing recipes.

Featuring **everyday ingredients** and step-by-step directions, these recipes make dinner a snap. And because they've all been **tested in the *Taste of Home* Test Kitchen**, you know each dish will turn out perfect! You'll even find **cooking tips** throughout the book in addition to a **photo with every recipe.**

Best of all, this one-of-a-kind cookbook offers recipes in **large print,** so you can simmer a winner with ease. With **Casseroles & One-Dish Meals** you're only moments away from sharing a **new family favorite!**

ROASTED KIELBASA
& VEGETABLES, 121

Corned Beef Hash
and Eggs, p. 19

CHAPTER 1

BREAKFAST & BRUNCH

Start the day with these sunny offerings.

Crab Quiche with Hollandaise

I discovered this quiche at a diner, and it was so amazing, I decided to duplicate it back at home. My family really loved the results.
—**AMY KNIGHT** LAKE LINDEN, MI

PREP: 25 MIN. • **BAKE:** 35 MIN.
MAKES: 6 SERVINGS (⅔ CUP SAUCE)

Pastry for single-crust pie (9 inches)
- 1 can (6 ounces) crabmeat, drained, flaked and cartilage removed
- 1 cup (4 ounces) shredded cheddar-Monterey Jack cheese
- ¾ cup frozen asparagus stir-fry vegetable blend, thawed
- ¼ cup finely chopped onion
- 3 eggs
- 1 cup evaporated milk
- ½ teaspoon salt
- ¼ teaspoon pepper
- ¼ teaspoon seafood seasoning
- ⅛ teaspoon hot pepper sauce

SAUCE
- 3 egg yolks
- 1 tablespoon water
- 1 tablespoon lemon juice
- ½ cup butter, melted
  Dash pepper

1. Roll out pastry to fit a 9-in. pie plate. Transfer pastry to pie plate. Trim pastry to ½ in. beyond edge of plate; flute the edges. Line unpricked pastry with a double thickness of heavy-duty foil. Bake at 450° for 8 minutes. Remove foil; bake 5 minutes longer. Place on a wire rack.

2. In a small bowl, combine the crab, cheese, vegetable blend and onion; transfer to crust. In another bowl, whisk the eggs, milk, salt, pepper, seafood seasoning and pepper sauce. Pour over crab mixture.

3. Bake at 375° for 35-40 minutes or until a knife inserted near the center comes out clean. Cover the edges with foil during the last 15 minutes to prevent overbrowning if necessary. Let stand for 5 minutes before cutting.

4. In a double boiler or metal bowl over simmering water, constantly whisk the egg yolks, water and lemon juice until mixture reaches 160° or is thick enough to coat the back of a metal spoon. Reduce the heat to low. Slowly drizzle in warm melted butter, whisking constantly. Whisk in pepper. Serve immediately with quiche.

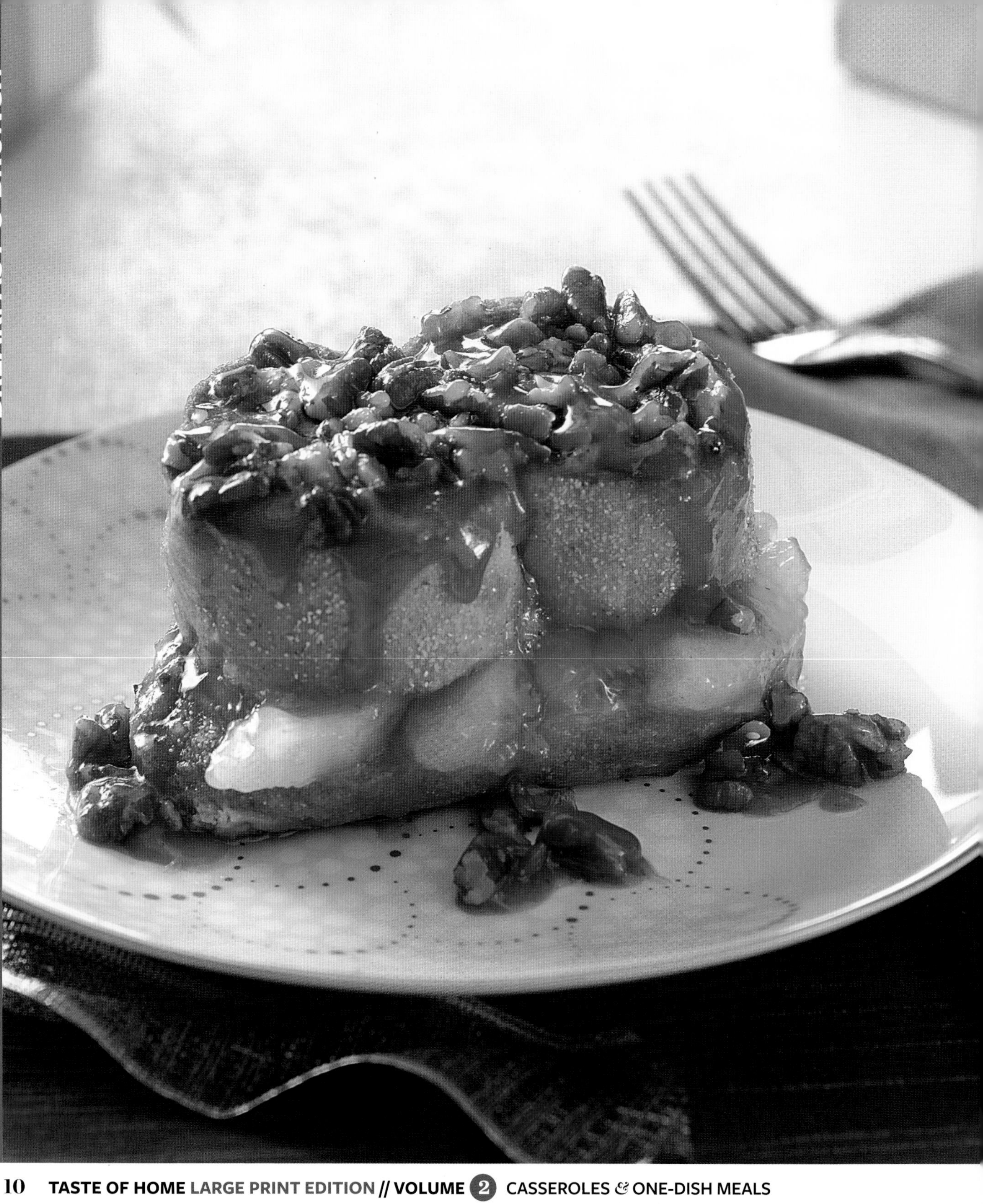

Baked Apple French Toast

This simply wonderful recipe will have folks requesting seconds. To make it extra special, I serve it with whipped topping, maple syrup and additional nuts.

—**BEVERLY JOHNSTON** RUBICON, WI

PREP: 20 MIN. + CHILLING • **BAKE:** 35 MIN.
MAKES: 10 SERVINGS

20	slices French bread (1 inch thick)
1	can (21 ounces) apple pie filling
8	eggs, lightly beaten
2	cups 2% milk
2	teaspoons vanilla extract
½	teaspoon ground cinnamon
½	teaspoon ground nutmeg

TOPPING

1	cup packed brown sugar
½	cup cold butter, cubed
1	cup chopped pecans
2	tablespoons corn syrup

1. Arrange 10 slices of bread in a greased 13x9-in. baking dish. Spread with pie filling; top with remaining bread. In a large bowl, whisk the eggs, milk, vanilla, cinnamon and nutmeg. Pour over bread. Cover and refrigerate overnight.

2. Remove from the refrigerator 30 minutes before baking. Meanwhile, place brown sugar in a small bowl. Cut in butter until mixture resembles coarse crumbs. Stir in pecans and corn syrup. Sprinkle over French toast.

3. Bake French toast, uncovered, at 350° for 35-40 minutes or until a knife inserted near the center comes out clean.

TOP TIP

When a recipe calls for lightly beaten eggs, you should beat an egg with a fork just until the yolk and white are combined. The mixture will look yellow.

Oven Denver Omelet

I like omelets but don't always have time to stand by the stove. That's why I often go for this oven-baked variety that I can quickly pop into the oven at a moment's notice. My family frequently requests this for Sunday brunch, and they always manage to empty the dish.

—ELLEN BOWER TANEYTOWN, MD

START TO FINISH: 30 MIN.
MAKES: 6 SERVINGS

8	eggs
1/2	cup half-and-half cream
1	cup (4 ounces) shredded cheddar cheese
1	cup finely chopped fully cooked ham
1/4	cup finely chopped green pepper
1/4	cup finely chopped onion

1. In a large bowl, whisk eggs and cream. Stir in the cheese, ham, green pepper and onion. Pour into a greased 9-in. square baking dish.

2. Bake at 400° for 25 minutes or until golden brown.

DID YOU KNOW?

While egg sizes can vary from small to jumbo, the cooks in the *Taste of Home* Test Kitchen use large eggs as the standard size for testing all *Taste of Home* recipes.

Greek Zucchini & Feta Bake

Looking to highlight your brunch with something light, indulgent and golden on top? Turn to this Greek-style egg bake.
—**GABRIELA STEFANESCU** WEBSTER, TX

PREP: 40 MIN. • **BAKE:** 30 MIN. + STANDING
MAKES: 12 SERVINGS

- 2 tablespoons olive oil, divided
- 5 medium zucchini, cut into 1/2-in. cubes (about 6 cups)
- 2 large onions, chopped (about 4 cups)
- 1 teaspoon dried oregano, divided
- 1/2 teaspoon salt
- 1/4 teaspoon pepper
- 6 eggs
- 2 teaspoons baking powder
- 1 cup (8 ounces) reduced-fat plain yogurt
- 1 cup all-purpose flour
- 2 packages (8 ounces each) feta cheese, cubed
- 1/4 cup minced fresh parsley
- 1 teaspoon paprika

1. Preheat oven to 350°. In a Dutch oven, heat 1 tablespoon oil over medium-high heat. Add half of the zucchini, half of the onions and 1/2 teaspoon oregano; cook and stir 8-10 minutes or until zucchini is crisp-tender. Remove from pan. Repeat with remaining vegetables. Stir in salt and pepper. Cool slightly.

2. In a large bowl, whisk eggs and baking powder until blended; whisk in yogurt and flour just until blended. Stir in cheese, parsley and zucchini mixture. Transfer to a greased 13x9-in. baking dish. Sprinkle with paprika.

3. Bake, uncovered, 30-35 minutes or until golden brown and set. Let stand 10 minutes before cutting.

NOTE If desired, thinly slice 1 medium zucchini and toss with 2 teaspoons olive oil; arrange over casserole before sprinkling with paprika. Bake as directed.

POTLUCK

Baked Blueberry & Peach Oatmeal

This oatmeal bake is a staple in our home. It's very easy to prepare the night before—just keep the dry and wet ingredients separate until ready to bake. I've tried a variety of fruits, but the blueberry and peach combo is our favorite.

—ROSEMARIE WELESKI NATRONA HEIGHTS, PA

PREP: 20 MIN. • **BAKE:** 35 MIN.
MAKES: 9 SERVINGS

3	cups old-fashioned oats
1/2	cup packed brown sugar
2	teaspoons baking powder
1/2	teaspoon salt
2	egg whites
1	egg
1 1/4	cups fat-free milk
1/4	cup canola oil
1	teaspoon vanilla extract
1	can (15 ounces) sliced peaches in juice, drained and chopped
1	cup fresh or frozen blueberries
1/3	cup chopped walnuts
	Additional fat-free milk, optional

1. In a large bowl, combine the oats, brown sugar, baking powder and salt. Whisk the egg whites, egg, milk, oil and vanilla; add to dry ingredients and stir until blended. Let stand for 5 minutes. Stir in peaches and blueberries.

2. Transfer to an 11x7-in. baking dish coated with cooking spray. Sprinkle with walnuts. Bake, uncovered, at 350° for 35-40 minutes or until top is lightly browned and a thermometer reads 160°. Serve with additional milk if desired.

DID YOU KNOW?

Old-fashioned oats and quick-cooking oats are interchangeable in recipes, as long as you consider the difference between the two. Both types of oats have been flattened with large rollers, but quick-cooking oats are cut into smaller pieces first. If you want a heartier texture, stick with old-fashioned oats. Quick-cooking oats, as their name suggests, cook faster, and they offer a more delicate texture.

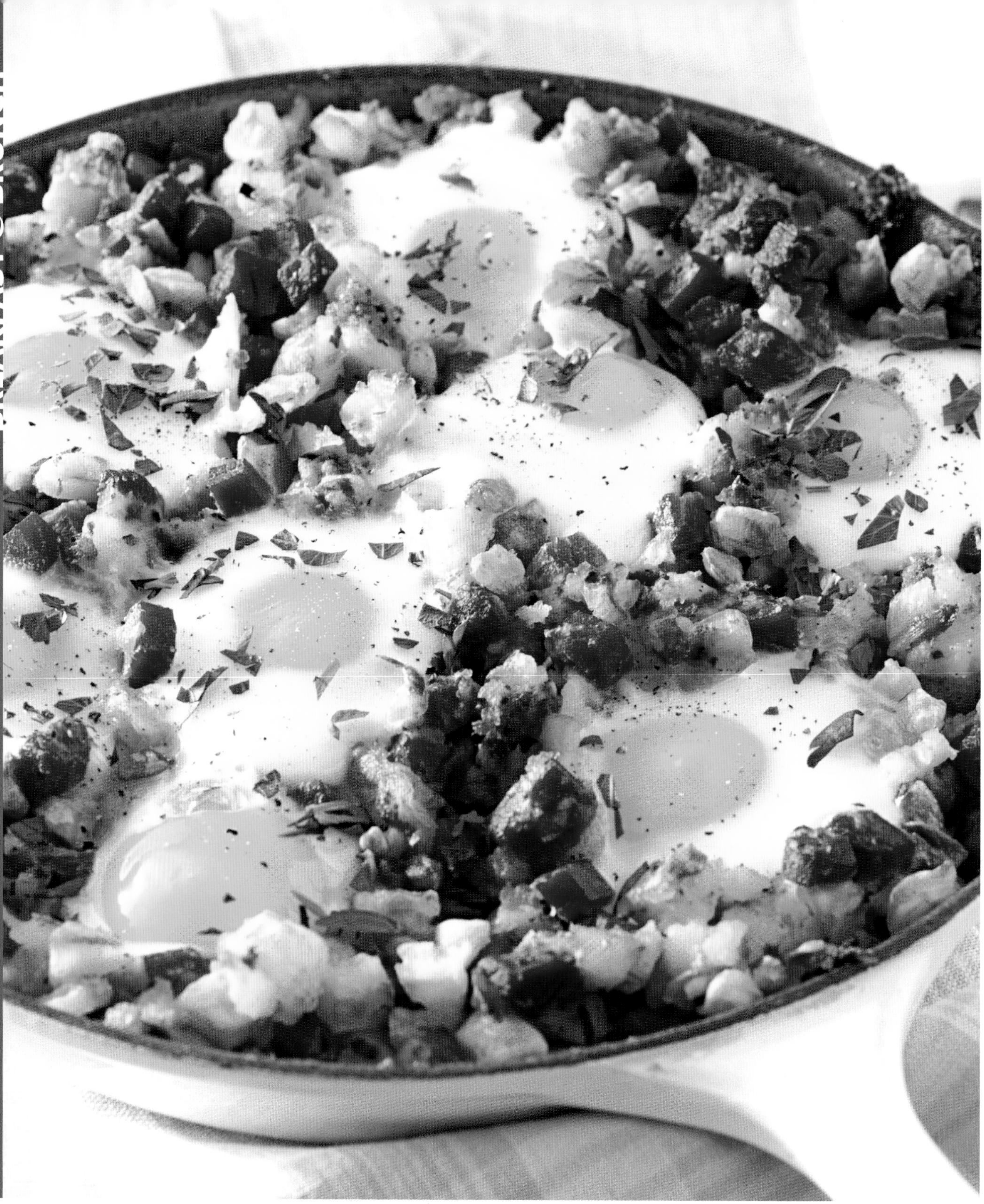

Corned Beef Hash and Eggs

Sunday breakfasts have always been special in our house. It's fun to get in the kitchen and cook with the kids. No matter how many new recipes we try, they always rate this No. 1.

—**RICK SKILDUM** MAPLE GROVE, MN

PREP: 15 MIN. • **BAKE:** 20 MIN.
MAKES: 8 SERVINGS

1	package (32 ounces) frozen cubed hash browns
1½	cups chopped onion
½	cup canola oil
4	to 5 cups chopped cooked corned beef
½	teaspoon salt
8	eggs
	Salt and pepper to taste
2	tablespoons minced fresh parsley

1. In a large ovenproof skillet, cook hash browns and onion in oil until potatoes are browned and onion is tender. Remove from heat; stir in corned beef and salt.

2. Make eight wells in the hash browns. Break one egg into each well. Sprinkle with salt and pepper. Cover and bake at 325° for 20-25 minutes or until eggs reach desired doneness. Garnish with parsley.

POTLUCK

Farmer's Strata

For an inexpensive and easy-to-prepare dish, try this hearty casserole. You can assemble it ahead of time and bake it just before folks arrive for your brunch. It includes tasty everyday ingredients such as bacon, cheese and potatoes.

—PAT KUETHER WESTMINSTER, CO

PREP: 25 MIN. + CHILLING • **BAKE:** 65 MIN.
MAKES: 16 SERVINGS

1	pound sliced bacon, cut into ½-inch pieces
2	cups chopped fully cooked ham
1	small onion, chopped
10	slices white bread, cubed
1	cup cubed cooked potatoes
3	cups (12 ounces) shredded cheddar cheese
8	eggs
3	cups milk
1	tablespoon Worcestershire sauce
1	teaspoon ground mustard
	Dash salt and pepper

1. In a large skillet, cook bacon over medium heat until crisp; add ham and onion. Cook and stir until the onion is tender; drain.

2. In a greased 13x9-in. baking dish, layer half the bread cubes, potatoes and cheese. Top with all of the bacon mixture. Repeat layers of bread, potatoes and cheese.

3. In a large bowl, beat the eggs; add the milk, Worcestershire sauce, mustard, salt and pepper. Pour over all. Cover and chill overnight.

4. Remove from refrigerator 30 minutes before baking. Bake strata, uncovered, at 325° for 65-70 minutes or until a knife inserted near the center comes out clean.

Bacon Vegetable Quiche

The best part about this recipe is you can tailor it to the season and use whatever veggies and cheese you happen to have on hand. I especially love this in spring with fresh greens and asparagus.

—SHANNON KOENE BLACKSBURG, VA

PREP: 25 MIN. • **BAKE:** 30 MIN.
MAKES: 6 SERVINGS

1 unbaked pastry shell (9 inches)
1 cup sliced fresh mushrooms
1 cup chopped fresh broccoli
¾ cup chopped sweet onion
2½ teaspoons olive oil
2 cups fresh baby spinach
3 eggs, lightly beaten
1 can (5 ounces) evaporated milk
1 tablespoon minced fresh rosemary or 1 teaspoon dried rosemary, crushed
¼ teaspoon salt
¼ teaspoon pepper
1 cup (4 ounces) shredded cheddar cheese
6 bacon strips, cooked and crumbled
½ cup crumbled tomato and basil feta cheese

1. Preheat oven to 450°. Line unpricked pastry shell with a double thickness of heavy-duty foil. Bake 8 minutes. Remove foil; bake 5 minutes longer. Reduce oven to 375°.

2. Meanwhile, in a large skillet, saute mushrooms, broccoli and onion in oil until tender. Add spinach; cook until wilted.

3. In a large bowl, whisk the eggs, milk, rosemary, salt and pepper. Stir in the vegetables, cheddar cheese and bacon. Pour into crust. Sprinkle with feta cheese.

4. Cover edges loosely with foil. Bake 30-35 minutes or until a knife inserted near the center comes out clean. Let stand 5 minutes before cutting.

FREEZE OPTION Cover and freeze unbaked quiche. To use, remove from freezer 30 minutes before baking (do not thaw). Preheat oven to 375°. Place quiche on a baking sheet; cover edges loosely with foil. Bake as directed, increasing time as necessary for a knife inserted near the center to come out clean.

POTLUCK

Broccoli Cheddar Casserole

In Arizona, we're lucky to have fresh produce all year.
I put broccoli to good use in this rich breakfast casserole.
—**CAROL STRICKLAND** YUMA, AZ

PREP: 15 MIN. • **BAKE:** 45 MIN. + STANDING
MAKES: 12-16 SERVINGS

8	cups chopped fresh broccoli
1	cup finely chopped onion
¾	cup butter, cubed
12	eggs
2	cups heavy whipping cream
2	cups (8 ounces) shredded cheddar cheese, divided
2	teaspoons salt
1	teaspoon pepper

1. In a large skillet over medium heat, saute broccoli and onion in butter until crisp-tender; set aside. In a large bowl, whisk the eggs, cream and 1¾ cups of the cheese. Stir in the broccoli mixture, salt and pepper. Pour into a greased 3-qt. baking dish; set in a large pan filled with 1 in. of hot water.

2. Bake, uncovered, at 350° for 45-50 minutes or until a knife inserted near the center comes out clean. Sprinkle with the remaining cheese. Let stand for 10 minutes before serving.

Easy Cheesy Loaded Grits

A classic bowl of grits inspired me to develop my own take filled with sausage, green chilies and cheeses. It just might be better than the original!

—JOAN HALLFORD FORT WORTH, TX

PREP: 35 MIN. • **BAKE:** 50 MIN. + STANDING
MAKES: 8 SERVINGS

- 1 pound mild or spicy bulk pork sausage
- 1 small onion, chopped
- 4 cups water
- ½ teaspoon salt
- 1 cup quick-cooking grits
- 3 cans (4 ounces each) chopped green chilies
- 1½ cups (6 ounces) shredded sharp cheddar cheese, divided
- 1½ cups (6 ounces) shredded Monterey Jack cheese, divided
- 2 tablespoons butter
- ¼ teaspoon hot pepper sauce
- 2 eggs, lightly beaten
- ¼ teaspoon paprika
  Chopped fresh cilantro

1. Preheat oven to 325°. In a large skillet, cook sausage and onion over medium heat 6-8 minutes or until sausage is no longer pink, breaking up sausage into crumbles; drain.

2. In a large saucepan, bring water and salt to a boil. Slowly stir in grits. Reduce heat to medium-low; cook, covered, about 5 minutes or until thickened, stirring occasionally. Remove from heat.

3. Add green chilies, ¾ cup cheddar cheese, ¾ cup Monterey Jack cheese, butter and pepper sauce; stir until cheese is melted. Stir in eggs, then sausage mixture.

4. Transfer to a greased 13x9-in. baking dish. Top with the remaining cheeses; sprinkle with paprika. Bake, uncovered, 50-60 minutes or until golden brown and set. Let stand 10 minutes before serving. Sprinkle with cilantro.

Berry-Topped Puff Pancake

This gorgeous pancake is surprisingly simple to make. Better yet, it's impressive to look at and to taste.

—MARIE COSENZA CORTLANDT MANOR, NY

PREP: 20 MIN. • **BAKE:** 15 MIN.
MAKES: 4 SERVINGS

 2 tablespoons butter
 2 eggs
 ½ cup 2% milk
 ½ cup all-purpose flour
 2 tablespoons sugar
 ¼ teaspoon salt

TOPPING
 ⅓ cup sugar
 1 tablespoon cornstarch
 ½ cup orange juice
 2 teaspoons orange liqueur
 1 cup sliced fresh strawberries
 1 cup fresh blueberries
 1 cup fresh raspberries
 Confectioners' sugar, optional

1. Place butter in a 9-in. pie plate. Place in a 425° oven for 4-5 minutes or until melted. Meanwhile, in a large bowl, whisk eggs and milk. In another bowl, combine the flour, sugar and salt. Whisk into egg mixture until blended. Pour into the prepared pie plate. Bake pancake for 14-16 minutes or until sides are crisp and golden brown.

2. Meanwhile, in a small saucepan, combine sugar and cornstarch. Gradually stir in orange juice and liqueur. Bring to a boil over medium heat, stirring constantly. Cook and stir 1-2 minutes longer or until thickened. Remove from the heat.

3. Spoon berries over pancake and drizzle with sauce. Dust with confectioners' sugar if desired.

**Triple Bean Bake
with Bacon, p. 48**

CHAPTER 2

SIDE DISHES

Round out meals with these oven-fresh favorites.

POTLUCK

Twice-Baked Cheddar Potato Casserole

Bacon, cheddar and sour cream turn ordinary potatoes into an extraordinary casserole. It's one of our family's beloved standards for the holidays.

—**KYLE COX** SCOTTSDALE, AZ

PREP: 70 MIN. • **BAKE:** 15 MIN.
MAKES: 12 SERVINGS (⅔ CUP EACH)

8	medium baking potatoes (about 8 ounces each)
½	cup butter, cubed
⅔	cup sour cream
⅔	cup 2% milk
1	teaspoon salt
¾	teaspoon pepper
10	bacon strips, cooked and crumbled, divided
2	cups (8 ounces) shredded cheddar cheese, divided
4	green onions, chopped, divided

1. Preheat oven to 425°. Scrub potatoes; pierce several times with a fork. Bake 45-60 minutes or until tender. Remove from oven; reduce oven setting to 350°.

2. When potatoes are cool enough to handle, cut each potato lengthwise in half. Scoop out pulp and place in a large bowl; discard shells. Mash pulp with butter; stir in the sour cream, milk, salt and pepper.

3. Reserve ¼ cup crumbled bacon for topping. Gently fold remaining bacon, 1 cup cheese and half of the green onions into potato mixture (do not overmix).

4. Transfer to a greased 11x7-in. baking dish. Top with the remaining cheese and green onions; sprinkle with reserved bacon. Bake 15-20 minutes or until heated through and cheese is melted.

TOP TIP

For fun individual servings, spoon the potato mixture into greased muffin cups instead of an 11x7-in. baking pan. Top with remaining ingredients as directed and bake 15 to 20 minutes or until heated through and cheese is melted. After removing from the oven, let stand 10 minutes before removing from cups.

Summer Squash Mushroom Casserole

With its crunchy topping, this rich and creamy side is a wonderful dish to take to potlucks and picnics. It pairs well with a variety of entrees.

—JENNIFER WALLACE CANAL WINCHESTER, OH

PREP: 20 MIN. • **BAKE:** 25 MIN.
MAKES: 10 SERVINGS

- 2 medium yellow summer squash, diced
- 1 large zucchini, diced
- 1/2 pound sliced fresh mushrooms
- 1 cup chopped onion
- 2 tablespoons olive oil
- 2 cups (8 ounces) shredded cheddar cheese
- 1 can (10¾ ounces) condensed cream of mushroom soup, undiluted
- 1/2 cup sour cream
- 1/2 teaspoon salt
- 1 cup crushed butter-flavored crackers (about 25 crackers)
- 1 tablespoon butter, melted

1. In a large skillet, saute the summer squash, zucchini, mushrooms and onion in oil until tender; drain.

2. In a large bowl, combine the vegetable mixture, cheese, soup, sour cream and salt. Transfer mixture to a greased 11x7-in. baking dish.

3. Combine the cracker crumbs and butter. Sprinkle over vegetable mixture.

4. Bake casserole, uncovered, at 350° for 25-30 minutes or until bubbly.

New Orleans-Style Scalloped Corn

This casserole is popular in New Orleans. I started making it years ago, and now my grown sons include it on their menus.
—**PRISCILLA GILBERT** INDIAN HARBOUR BEACH, FL

PREP: 20 MIN. • **BAKE:** 35 MIN.
MAKES: 8 SERVINGS

- 4 teaspoons butter
- 1 large onion, finely chopped
- 1 large sweet red pepper, finely chopped
- 4 cups frozen corn
- 2 eggs
- 1 cup fat-free milk
- 1 tablespoon sugar
- 1 to 2 teaspoons hot pepper sauce
- 1/2 teaspoon dried thyme
- 1/4 teaspoon salt
- 1/4 teaspoon pepper
- 1 1/4 cups crushed reduced-fat butter-flavored crackers (about 30 crackers)
- 5 green onions, sliced

1. Preheat oven to 350°. In a large skillet, heat butter over medium-high heat. Add onion and pepper; cook and stir until tender. Add corn; heat through, stirring occasionally. Remove from heat.

2. In a small bowl, whisk eggs, milk, sugar, pepper sauce, thyme, salt and pepper; add to corn mixture. Stir in crushed crackers and green onions.

3. Transfer to a 2-qt. baking dish coated with cooking spray. Bake, uncovered, 35-40 minutes or until a knife inserted near the center comes out clean.

Broccoli and Carrot Cheese Bake

A creamy sauce flavored with cheese makes vegetables so much more appealing to my crowd. This side dish will please even the pickiest veggie-phobics. It uses vegetables that are available year-round, so it works for spring as well as winter meals.

—TRISHA KRUSE EAGLE, ID

PREP: 25 MIN. • **BAKE:** 30 MIN. + STANDING
MAKES: 9 SERVINGS

- 2 cups thinly sliced fresh carrots
- 2 cups fresh broccoli florets
- 3 eggs
- 2 cups 2% milk
- 1/4 cup butter, melted
- 1/2 teaspoon salt
- 1/4 teaspoon ground nutmeg
- 1/4 teaspoon pepper
- 1 1/2 cups (6 ounces) grated Gruyere or Swiss cheese, divided
- 6 cups cubed egg bread

1. Place carrots and broccoli in a steamer basket; place in a large saucepan over 1 in. of water. Bring to a boil; cover and steam 3-4 minutes or until crisp-tender.

2. Preheat oven to 325°. In a large bowl, whisk eggs, milk, butter, salt, nutmeg and pepper. Stir in vegetables and 1 cup cheese. Gently stir in bread.

3. Transfer to a greased 11x7-in. baking dish; sprinkle with remaining cheese. Bake, uncovered, 30-35 minutes or until a knife inserted near the center comes out clean. Let stand 10 minutes before serving.

TO MAKE AHEAD This recipe can be made a day ahead; cover and refrigerate. Remove from the refrigerator 30 minutes before baking. Bake as directed.

Saucy Green Bean Bake

Here's a different way to serve green beans. It's a nice change of pace from plain veggies, yet it doesn't require much work on your part. Keep it in mind the next time your schedule is full and you have to get dinner on the table fast.

—**JUNE FORMANEK** BELLE PLAINE, IA

START TO FINISH: 30 MIN.
MAKES: 4-6 SERVINGS

1	can (8 ounces) tomato sauce
2	tablespoons diced pimientos
1	tablespoon prepared mustard
1/4	teaspoon salt
1/8	teaspoon pepper
1	pound fresh or frozen cut green beans, cooked
1/2	cup chopped onion
1/3	cup chopped green pepper
1	garlic clove, minced
2	tablespoons butter
3/4	cup cubed process cheese (Velveeta)

1. In a large bowl, combine the first five ingredients. Add the green beans; toss to coat. Transfer to an ungreased 1-qt. baking dish. Cover and bake at 350° for 20 minutes.

2. Meanwhile, in a large skillet, saute the onion, green pepper and garlic in butter until tender. Sprinkle over beans. Top with cheese. Bake, uncovered, for 3-5 minutes or until cheese is melted.

TOP TIP

Process cheese is a blend of different cheeses that is similar in flavor to the natural cheese from which it's made. Generally, it is stable at room temperature. Process cheese is a mainstay for many busy family cooks because it stays smooth and creamy when it is heated, making it an easy way to jazz up side dishes. The most common brand name of process American cheese is Velveeta.

Three-Cheese Hash Brown Bake

Serve up comfort food with this cheesy casserole featuring convenient frozen hash browns. It requires just 10 minutes of prep before you pop it in the oven. It's perfect for breakfast but a welcomed addition to any meal.

—NANCY SIDHU FRANKLIN, WI

PREP: 10 MIN. • **BAKE:** 55 MIN. + STANDING
MAKES: 12 SERVINGS

- 2 cans (10¾ ounces each) condensed cream of potato soup, undiluted
- 1 cup (8 ounces) sour cream
- 1 teaspoon garlic powder
- ½ teaspoon pepper
- 1 package (32 ounces) frozen cubed hash brown potatoes, thawed
- 2 cups (8 ounces) shredded cheddar cheese
- 1 cup grated Parmesan cheese
- ½ cup shredded Swiss cheese

1. Preheat oven to 350°. In a large bowl, mix soup, sour cream, garlic powder and pepper until blended. Stir in remaining ingredients.

2. Transfer to a greased 13x9-in. baking dish. Bake, uncovered, 55-65 minutes or until golden brown and potatoes are tender. Let stand 10 minutes before serving.

Sausage and Rice Casserole Side Dish

When company's coming or I need a quick-and-easy dish to pass, this is my hands-down favorite. A neighbor introduced me to the delicious combination of fluffy rice and sage-seasoned sausage. One forkful was all it took to convince me I'd found a winner.

—JOYCE GREEN BETTENRDORF, IA

PREP: 15 MIN. • **BAKE:** 1 HOUR
MAKES: 6 SERVINGS

1	pound sage-flavored pork sausage
1	cup sliced celery
$1/2$	cup chopped onion
$1/4$	cup chopped sweet red pepper
$1/4$	cup chopped green pepper
$1/2$	cup fresh mushrooms, sliced
1	can (8 ounces) sliced water chestnuts, drained
1	cup converted rice, uncooked
2	cups chicken broth
$1/2$	teaspoon salt
$1/8$	teaspoon ground pepper

1. Brown sausage in heavy skillet over medium heat; transfer sausage to a $2^{1/2}$-qt. greased casserole dish. In the sausage drippings, saute celery, onion, peppers and mushrooms until lightly browned; transfer to casserole dish.

2. Add water chestnuts, rice, broth and seasonings to casserole dish; mix well. Cover tightly and bake at 350° for 1 to $1^{1/2}$ hours or until rice is fluffy and tender.

TOP TIP

Also called parboiled rice, converted rice is the unhulled grain that has been steam-pressured before milling. This process retains nutrients and makes fluffy separated grains of rice. It is neither regular long grain rice nor instant long grain rice. Converted rice takes slightly longer to cook than regular long grain rice.

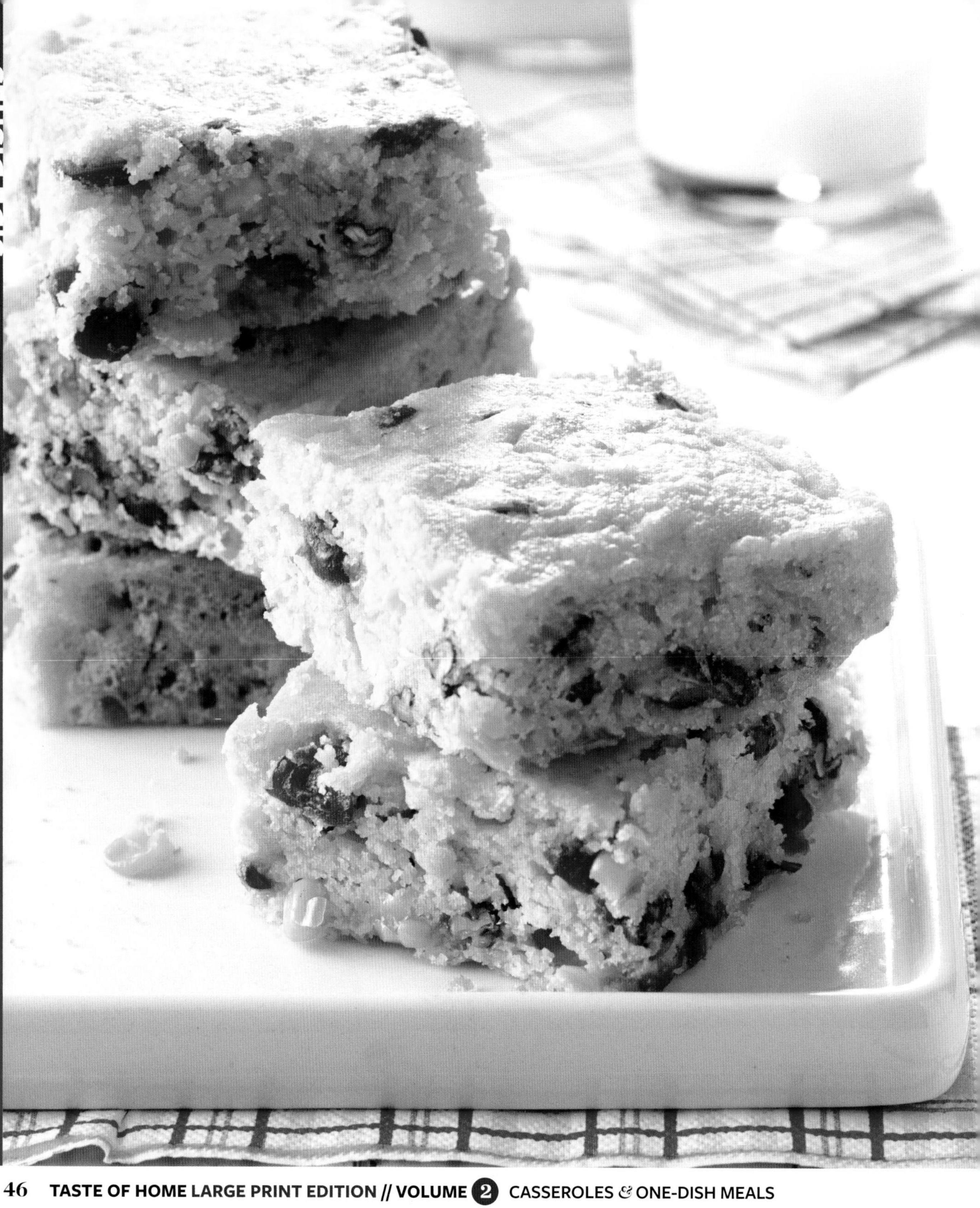

Cranberry Corn Bread Casserole

What could be better on a cold day than a warm casserole of creamy sweet corn bread? Since it starts with a mix, this side takes no time to make. Just bake, scoop and eat. Yum!

—**VALERY ANDERSON** STERLING HEIGHTS, MI

PREP: 15 MIN. • **BAKE:** 20 MIN.
MAKES: 9 SERVINGS

- ½ cup dried cranberries
- ½ cup boiling water
- 1 package (8½ ounces) corn bread/muffin mix
- 1 teaspoon onion powder
- ¼ teaspoon rubbed sage
- 1 egg
- 1 can (14¾ ounces) cream-style corn
- 2 tablespoons butter, melted
- ¼ cup chopped pecans
- ½ teaspoon grated orange peel

1. Place cranberries in a small bowl; cover with boiling water. Let stand for 5 minutes; drain and set aside.

2. In a small bowl, combine the muffin mix, onion powder and sage.

3. In another bowl, whisk the egg, corn and butter; stir into dry ingredients just until moistened. Fold in the pecans, orange peel and cranberries.

4. Transfer to a greased 8-in.-square baking dish. Bake uncovered at 400° for 20-25 minutes or until set.

FREEZE OPTION Cool baked corn bread in pan; cover and freeze. To use, partially thaw in refrigerator overnight. Remove from refrigerator 30 minutes before baking. Preheat oven to 350°. Reheat the corn bread 10-12 minutes or until heated through.

Triple Bean Bake with Bacon

Ordinary baked beans become extraordinary when you mix bean varieties and add the zing of horseradish.

—SHERRI MELOTIK OAK CREEK, WI

PREP: 15 MIN. • **BAKE:** 30 MIN.
MAKES: 8 SERVINGS

- ½ pound bacon strips, cut into ½-inch pieces
- ⅔ cup chopped onion (about 1 medium)
- 1 can (15½ ounces) great northern beans, undrained
- 1 can (16 ounces) butter beans, rinsed and drained
- 1 can (16 ounces) kidney beans, rinsed and drained
- ¾ cup packed brown sugar
- 1 tablespoon prepared horseradish
- 1 tablespoon yellow mustard

1. In a Dutch oven, cook bacon over medium heat until crisp. Remove to paper towels with a slotted spoon; drain, reserving 1 tablespoon drippings. Add onion to drippings; cook and stir over medium heat until tender.

2. Stir in the remaining ingredients; return bacon to pan. Transfer to a greased 2-qt. baking dish. Cover and bake at 325° for 30-35 minutes or until heated through. Uncover and bake until desired consistency.

Brussels Sprouts au Gratin

In our house, Brussels sprouts have always been popular. When I topped them with a creamy sauce, Swiss cheese and bread crumbs, the dish became a new tradition for special dinners.
—GWEN GREGORY RIO OSO, CA

PREP: 30 MIN. • **BAKE:** 20 MIN.
MAKES: 6 SERVINGS

- 2 pounds fresh Brussels sprouts, quartered
- 1 tablespoon olive oil
- ½ teaspoon salt, divided
- ¼ teaspoon pepper, divided
- ¾ cup cubed sourdough or French bread
- 1 tablespoon butter
- 1 tablespoon minced fresh parsley
- 2 garlic cloves, coarsely chopped
- 1 cup heavy whipping cream
- ⅛ teaspoon crushed red pepper flakes
- ⅛ teaspoon ground nutmeg
- ½ cup shredded white sharp cheddar or Swiss cheese

1. Preheat oven to 450°. Place the Brussels sprouts in a large bowl. Add oil, ¼ teaspoon salt and ⅛ teaspoon pepper; toss to coat. Transfer to two ungreased 15x10-in. baking pans. Roast sprouts 8-10 minutes or until lightly browned and crisp-tender. Reduce the oven setting to 400°.

2. Meanwhile, place bread, butter, parsley and garlic in a food processor; pulse until fine crumbs form.

3. Place roasted sprouts in a greased 8-in.-square baking dish. In a small bowl, mix cream, pepper flakes, nutmeg, and remaining salt and pepper. Pour over Brussels sprouts; sprinkle with cheese.

4. Top with crumb mixture. Bake, uncovered, 15-20 minutes or until bubbly and topping is lightly browned.

Eggnog Sweet Potato Bake

I love eggnog so I am always looking for new ways to use it. When I added it to mashed sweet potatoes, I knew I had a winner. You can make this the night before and refrigerate it unbaked; the next day, let it stand at room temperature for 30 minutes before baking.

—KATIE WOLLGAST FLORISSANT, MO

PREP: 1¼ HOURS + COOLING
BAKE: 30 MIN.
MAKES: 8 SERVINGS

3½ pounds sweet potatoes (about 5 large)
⅔ cup eggnog
½ cup golden raisins
2 tablespoons sugar
1 teaspoon salt

TOPPING

¼ cup all-purpose flour
¼ cup quick-cooking oats
¼ cup packed brown sugar
¼ cup chopped pecans
½ teaspoon ground cinnamon
¼ teaspoon ground nutmeg
2 tablespoons butter, melted

1. Preheat oven to 400°. Scrub sweet potatoes; pierce several times with a fork. Place on a foil-lined 15x10-in. baking pan; bake 1 hour or until tender. Remove from oven. Reduce oven setting to 350°.

2. When potatoes are cool enough to handle, remove and discard peel. Mash potatoes in a large bowl (you should have about 6 cups mashed). Stir in eggnog, raisins, sugar and salt. Transfer to a greased 11x7-in. baking dish.

3. For topping, in a small bowl, mix flour, oats, brown sugar, pecans and spices; stir in butter. Sprinkle over sweet potatoes. Bake, uncovered, 30-35 minutes or until heated through and the topping is lightly browned.

NOTE This recipe was tested with commercially prepared eggnog.

Roasted Cauliflower Mash

Here's a tempting yet lower-carb alternative to traditional side dishes of spuds or rice. Guests might even say this standout cauliflower tastes like mashed potatoes.
—**JANE MCGLOTHREN** DAPHNE, AL

PREP: 30 MIN. • **BAKE:** 25 MIN.
MAKES: 10 SERVINGS

- 2 medium heads cauliflower, broken into florets
- 1/4 cup olive oil
- 6 garlic cloves, minced
- 2 teaspoons Greek seasoning
- 1 cup (4 ounces) shredded sharp cheddar cheese
- 2/3 cup sour cream
- 1/2 cup crumbled cooked bacon
- 1/3 cup butter, cubed

1. In a large bowl, combine the cauliflower, oil, garlic and Greek seasoning. Transfer to a greased 15x10-in. baking pan. Bake, uncovered, at 425° for 15-20 minutes or until tender, stirring occasionally.

2. Transfer cauliflower to a large bowl. Mash cauliflower with cheese, sour cream, bacon and butter. Transfer to a greased 8-in.-square baking dish. Bake at 350° for 25-30 minutes or until heated through.

Midwest Meatball
Casserole, p. 62

CHAPTER 3

BEEF & GROUND BEEF

These meaty bakes will satisfy even the heartiest appetites.

Favorite Baked Spaghetti

Layering the pasta and sauce ensures your spaghetti won't dry out if you transport it to an event. People of all ages dig right in—my grandkids especially like the gooey cheese.
—**LOUISE MILLER** WESTMINSTER, MD

PREP: 25 MIN. • **BAKE:** 1 HOUR
MAKES: 10 SERVINGS

1	package (16 ounces) spaghetti
1	pound ground beef
1	medium onion, chopped
1	jar (24 ounces) meatless spaghetti sauce
1/2	teaspoon seasoned salt
2	eggs
1/3	cup grated Parmesan cheese
5	tablespoons butter, melted
2	cups (16 ounces) 4% cottage cheese
4	cups (16 ounces) part-skim shredded mozzarella cheese

1. Cook the spaghetti according to the package directions. Meanwhile, in a large skillet, cook beef and onion over medium heat until the meat is no longer pink, breaking the meat into crumbles; drain. Stir in the spaghetti sauce and seasoned salt; set aside.

2. In a large bowl, whisk eggs, Parmesan cheese and butter. Drain the spaghetti; add to the egg mixture and toss to coat.

3. Place half of the spaghetti mixture in a greased 3-qt. baking dish. Top with half of the cottage cheese, meat sauce and mozzarella cheese. Repeat layers.

4. Cover and bake at 350° for 40 minutes. Uncover; bake 20-25 minutes longer or until cheese is melted.

TOP TIP

An opened block of mozzarella cheese should be wrapped with waxed paper, then wrapped again with a tight seal of plastic wrap or foil. Stored this way at a temperature of 34° to 38° in the refrigerator, mozzarella cheese will keep for several weeks. If mold develops, trim off the mold plus an extra 1/2 inch of cheese and discard it. The rest of the cheese may be eaten.

Beef Stew with Sesame Seed Biscuits

Comfort food fills you up body and soul. That's what this oven stew is all about!

—LINDA BACCI LIVONIA, NY

PREP: 20 MIN. + SIMMERING • **BAKE:** 30 MIN.
MAKES: 5 SERVINGS

1 pound beef stew meat, cut into 1-inch cubes
2 tablespoons olive oil
1½ cups chopped onions
1 cup chopped celery
1 garlic clove, minced
1 tablespoon all-purpose flour
1½ cups water
1 cup diced tomatoes
½ cup Burgundy wine or beef broth
⅓ cup tomato paste
1 tablespoon sugar
¾ teaspoon salt
½ teaspoon Worcestershire sauce
¼ teaspoon pepper
2 cups cubed peeled potatoes
2 cups sliced fresh carrots
1 can (4 ounces) mushroom stems and pieces, drained
¼ cup sour cream

SESAME SEED BISCUITS

1¼ cups all-purpose flour
2 teaspoons baking powder
½ teaspoon salt
¼ cup shortening
¾ cup sour cream
2 tablespoons 2% milk
1 tablespoon sesame seeds

1. In a Dutch oven, brown the beef in oil in batches. Remove and keep warm. In same pan, saute onions and celery until tender. Add garlic; cook 1 minute longer.

2. Stir in flour until blended. Gradually add water; stir in tomatoes, wine, tomato paste, sugar, salt, Worcestershire sauce, pepper and beef. Bring to a boil. Reduce heat; cover and simmer 1¼ hours.

3. Add the potatoes and carrots; cook 30-45 minutes longer or until beef and vegetables are tender. Stir in mushrooms and sour cream. Transfer to a greased 13x9-in. baking dish.

4. Preheat oven to 400°. For the biscuits, in a large bowl, combine the flour, baking powder and salt. Cut in shortening until mixture resembles coarse crumbs. Stir in sour cream just until moistened.

5. Turn the dough onto a lightly floured surface; knead 8-10 times. Roll out to ½-in. thickness; cut with a floured 2-in. biscuit cutter. Brush with milk; sprinkle with sesame seeds. Arrange over stew.

6. Bake 30-35 minutes or until biscuits are golden brown.

Midwest Meatball Casserole

I've often relied on my meatball casserole as a satisfying sit-down meal at the end of a long day. I usually have all the ingredients on hand—no extra shopping trip needed!

—JUDY LARSON GREENDALE, WI

PREP: 15 MIN. • **BAKE:** 30 MIN.
MAKES: 6 SERVINGS

- 2 cans (8 ounces each) tomato sauce, divided
- 1 egg
- ¼ cup dry bread crumbs
- ¼ cup chopped onion
- 1 teaspoon salt
- 1 pound lean ground beef (90% lean)
- 1 package (10 ounces) frozen mixed vegetables
- ½ teaspoon dried thyme
- ⅛ teaspoon pepper
- 1 package (16 ounces) frozen shredded hash brown potatoes, thawed
- 1 tablespoon butter, melted
- 3 slices process American cheese slices, cut into ½-inch strips

1. In a large bowl, combine 2 tablespoons tomato sauce, egg, bread crumbs, onion and salt. Crumble beef over mixture and mix well. Shape into 1-in. balls.

2. Place the meatballs on a greased rack in a shallow baking pan and bake at 375° for 15-20 minutes or until meatballs are no longer pink; drain.

3. Meanwhile, in a large skillet, combine the remaining tomato sauce with the vegetables and seasonings. Cover and simmer 10-15 minutes or until heated through; stir in meatballs and set aside.

4. Place potatoes in a greased 11x7-in. baking dish. Brush with butter and bake at 375° for 15-20 minutes or until lightly browned. Remove from oven; top with meatball mixture. Arrange cheese in a lattice pattern on top. Bake, uncovered, for 20-25 minutes longer or until heated through and cheese is melted.

Quick & Easy Deep-Dish Pizza

Years ago when I was trying to impress my boyfriend with my cooking, I made a meaty deep-dish pizza. I think it worked. He's now my husband—and I still prepare it for our family at least once a month!

—STACEY WHITE FUQUAY-VARINA, NC

PREP: 30 MIN. • **BAKE:** 30 MIN.
MAKES: 8 SERVINGS

- 1 pound ground beef
- 1 medium green pepper, chopped
- 1 small onion, chopped
- 1 jar (14 ounces) pizza sauce
- 10 slices Canadian bacon (about 6 ounces), coarsely chopped
- 2 packages (6½ ounces each) pizza crust mix
- 2 cups (8 ounces) shredded part-skim mozzarella cheese
- 4 ounces sliced pepperoni

1. Preheat oven to 425°. In a large skillet, cook the beef, pepper and onion over medium heat 8-10 minutes or until beef is no longer pink, breaking up beef into crumbles; drain. Stir in pizza sauce and Canadian bacon; remove from heat.

2. Prepare the dough for pizza crust according to the package directions. Press dough to fit bottom and 1 in. up sides of a greased 13x9-in. baking pan.

3. Spoon the meat sauce into the crust. Sprinkle with cheese; top with pepperoni. Bake, covered, 25 minutes. Uncover; bake 5-10 minutes longer or until the crust and cheese are golden brown.

FREEZE OPTION Cool meat sauce before assembling the pizza. Securely cover and freeze unbaked pizza. To use, bake frozen pizza, covered with foil, in a preheated 425° oven 25 minutes. Uncover; bake 15-20 minutes longer or until golden brown and heated through.

Ravioli Lasagna

When people sample this, they think it's a from-scratch recipe. But the lasagna actually starts with frozen ravioli and requires just three other ingredients. How easy is that?
—**PATRICIA SMITH** ASHEBORO, NC

PREP: 25 MIN. • **BAKE:** 40 MIN.
MAKES: 6 - 8 SERVINGS

- 1   pound ground beef
- 1   jar (28 ounces) spaghetti sauce
- 1   package (25 ounces) frozen sausage or cheese ravioli
- 1½ cups (6 ounces) shredded part-skim mozzarella cheese

1. In a large skillet, cook the beef over medium heat until no longer pink, breaking into crumbles; drain. In a greased 2 ½ qt. baking dish, layer a third of the spaghetti sauce, half of the ravioli and beef and ½ cup cheese; repeat layers. Top with remaining sauce and cheese.

2. Cover and bake at 400° for 40-45 minutes or until heated through.

> **TOP TIP**
>
> Bringing a casserole to a potluck but don't have a casserole carrier? Set the dish inside a clear plastic oven bag and close it with a twist tie. The bag will trap any spills, it won't melt and the potluck organizers will be able to see what's inside. Then wrap the dish in a thick beach towel to keep the food warm if you are traveling a short distance. For long distances, place the cooled dish on ice and reheat at the party.

Reuben Quiche

Classic Reuben sandwich ingredients make this hearty quiche taste like a deli specialty. Serve Thousand Island dressing on the side.

—BARBARA NOWAKOWSKI

NORTH TONAWANDA, NY

PREP: 25 MIN. • **BAKE:** 25 MIN.
MAKES: 6 SERVINGS

- 1 cup plus 3 tablespoons finely crushed Rye Triscuits or other crackers
- 1 tablespoon rye or all-purpose flour
- 2 tablespoons plus 1½ teaspoons butter, melted

FILLING

- 5 green onions, chopped
- 1 tablespoon butter
- 1½ cups (6 ounces) shredded Swiss cheese, divided
- 1 package (2½ ounces) deli corned beef, cut into 2-inch strips
- ½ cup sauerkraut, well drained
- 4 eggs
- 1 cup half-and-half cream
- 1 tablespoon all-purpose flour
- ½ teaspoon ground mustard
- ¼ teaspoon salt

1. In a small bowl, combine the cracker crumbs, flour and butter; press onto bottom and up sides of an ungreased 9-in. pie plate. Bake at 375° for 8-10 minutes or until edges are lightly browned.

2. Meanwhile, in a small skillet, saute onions in butter until tender; set aside. Sprinkle ½ cup cheese over the crust. Top with the corned beef, sauerkraut and remaining cheese. Whisk the eggs, cream, flour, mustard, salt and reserved onion mixture; pour over cheese.

3. Bake quiche, uncovered, at 375° for 25-30 minutes or until a knife inserted near the center comes out clean. Let stand for 5 minutes before cutting.

HOW TO

MAKE CRACKER CRUMBS

❶ Place the crackers in a heavy-duty resealable plastic bag. Seal the bag, pushing out as much air as possible.

❷ Press a rolling pin over the bag, crushing the crackers to fine crumbs. You can also make crumbs using a blender or food processor.

FREEZE IT

Cheddar Beef Enchiladas

Trying to satisfy several picky eaters in our house, I came up with my beef enchiladas. They were a hit with everyone! I usually fix two pans at once and freeze the second one for an especially busy day.

—**STACY CIZEK** CONRAD, IA

PREP: 30 MIN. • **BAKE:** 20 MIN.
MAKES: 2 CASSEROLES
(5-6 ENCHILADAS EACH)

- 1 pound ground beef
- 1 envelope taco seasoning
- 1 cup water
- 2 cups cooked rice
- 1 can (16 ounces) refried beans
- 2 cups (8 ounces) shredded cheddar cheese, divided
- 10 to 12 flour tortillas (8 inches), warmed
- 1 jar (16 ounces) salsa
- 1 can (10¾ ounces) condensed cream of chicken soup, undiluted

1. In a large skillet, cook ground beef over medium heat until no longer pink, breaking the beef into crumbles; drain. Stir in the taco seasoning and water. Bring to a boil. Reduce heat; simmer, uncovered, for 5 minutes. Stir in rice. Cook and stir until liquid is evaporated.

2. Spread about 2 tablespoons beans, ¼ cup beef mixture and 1 tablespoon cheddar cheese down the center of each tortilla; roll up. Place seam side down in two greased 13x9-in. baking dishes.

3. Combine salsa and soup; pour down the center of enchiladas. Sprinkle with remaining cheese.

4. Bake one casserole, uncovered, at 350° for 20-25 minutes or until heated through and cheese is melted. Cover and freeze remaining casserole for up to 3 months.

TO USE FROZEN CASSEROLE Thaw the casserole in refrigerator overnight. Cover and bake at 350° for 30 minutes. Uncover; bake 5-10 minutes longer or until heated through and cheese is melted.

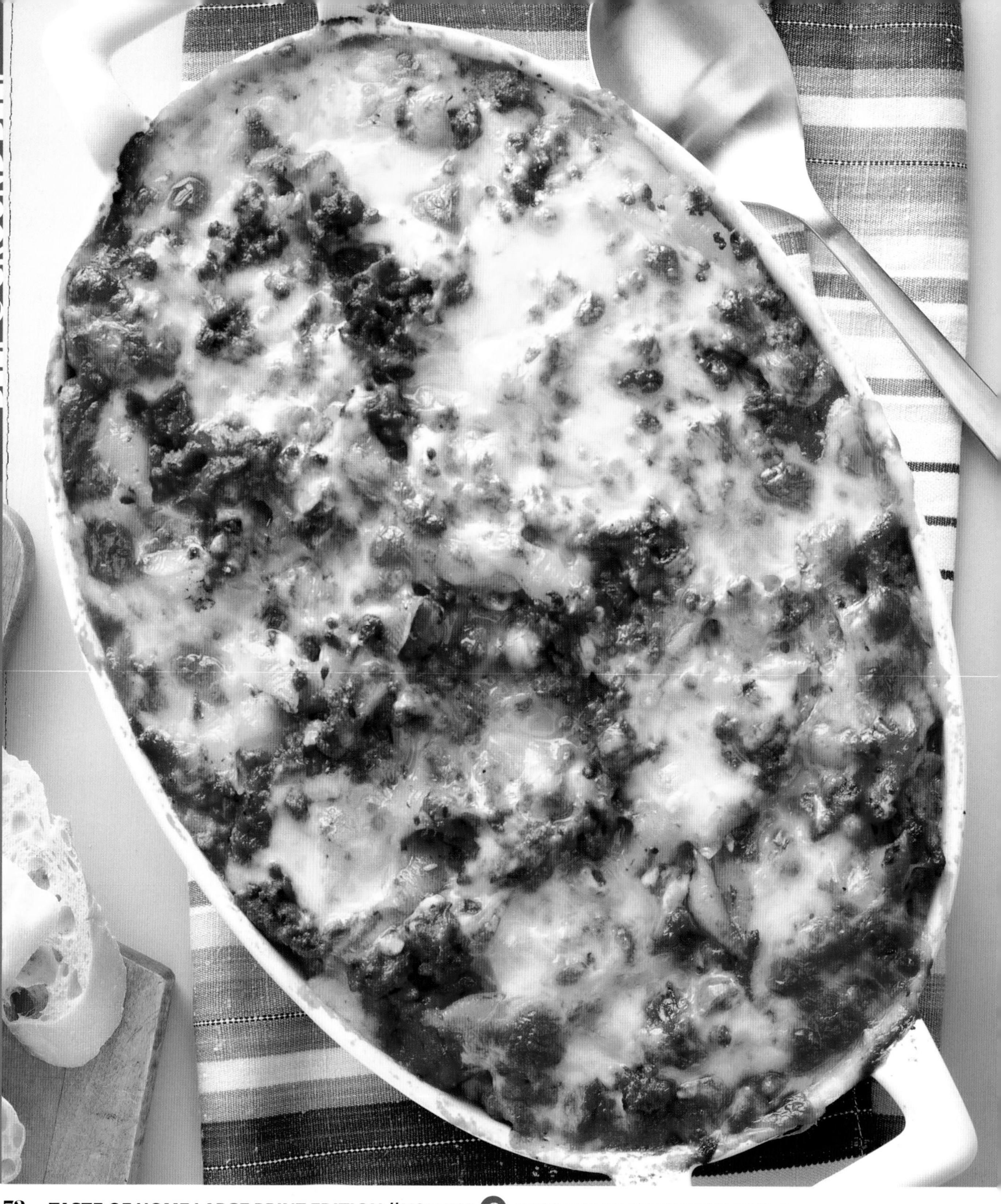

Lasagna Casserole

When I was a child, I always asked for this yummy dinner on my birthday. My mother made the sauce from scratch, but I use the store-bought kind to save time. For extra spice, replace the beef with Italian sausage.
—**DEB MORRISON** SKIATOOK, OK

PREP: 15 MIN. • **BAKE:** 1 HOUR + STANDING
MAKES: 6-8 SERVINGS

1   pound ground beef
¼   cup chopped onion
½   teaspoon salt
½   teaspoon pepper, divided
1   pound medium pasta shells, cooked and drained
4   cups (16 ounces) shredded part-skim mozzarella cheese, divided
3   cups (24 ounces) 4% cottage cheese
2   eggs, lightly beaten
⅓   cup grated Parmesan cheese
2   tablespoons dried parsley flakes
1   jar (24 ounces) meatless pasta sauce

1. In a large skillet, cook beef and onion over medium heat until meat is no longer pink, breaking meat into crumbles; drain. Sprinkle with the salt and ¼ teaspoon pepper; set aside.

2. In a large bowl, combine pasta, 3 cups mozzarella cheese, cottage cheese, eggs, Parmesan cheese, parsley and remaining pepper. Transfer to a greased shallow 3-qt. baking dish. Top with beef mixture and pasta sauce (dish will be full).

3. Cover and bake at 350° for 45 minutes. Sprinkle with the remaining mozzarella cheese. Bake, uncovered, 15 minutes longer or until bubbly and mozzarella cheese is melted. Let casserole stand for 10 minutes before serving.

FREEZE OPTION Sprinkle the casserole with the remaining mozzarella cheese. Cover and freeze the unbaked casserole. To use, partially thaw in the refrigerator overnight. Remove from the refrigerator 30 minutes before baking. Preheat the oven to 350°. Bake casserole as directed, increasing the time as necessary to heat through and for a thermometer inserted in the center to read 165°.

Garlic Pot Roast

My family loves garlic—the more, the better! So I created a pot roast that gets twice the flavor from both garlic cloves and powder. Now, I regularly serve this for Sunday dinner. The tender beef, potatoes, onion and carrots make a complete and satisfying meal.

—**RHONDA HAMPTON** COOKEVILLE, TN

PREP: 20 MIN. • **BAKE:** 2½ HOURS
MAKES: 8 SERVINGS

- 1   boneless beef chuck roast (3 pounds)
- 4   garlic cloves, peeled and halved
- 3   teaspoons garlic powder
- 3   teaspoons Italian salad dressing mix
- ½   teaspoon pepper
- 1   tablespoon canola oil
- 3   cups water
- 1   envelope onion soup mix
- 1   teaspoon reduced-sodium beef bouillon granules
- 5   medium potatoes, peeled and quartered
- 1   pound fresh baby carrots
- 1   large onion, cut into 1-inch pieces

1. Using the point of a sharp knife, make eight slits in the roast. Insert garlic into slits. Combine the garlic powder, salad dressing mix and pepper; rub over roast. In a Dutch oven, brown roast in oil on all sides; drain.

2. Combine the water, onion soup mix and bouillon; pour over roast. Cover and bake at 325° for 1½ hours.

3. Add the potatoes, carrots and onion. Cover and bake 1 hour longer or until the meat and vegetables are tender. Thicken pan juices if desired.

TOP TIP

Store whole or partial garlic bulbs in a cool, dry, dark place in a well-ventilated container, such as a mesh bag, for up to 2 months. To help prevent them from drying out, leave the cloves on the bulb with the skin attached. Do not refrigerate because they have a tendency to sprout, which can give them a bitter flavor.

Spicy Nacho Bake

When I needed to bring a dish to a dinner meeting, I chose my nacho bake. Since then, I've been getting requests for it whenever there's a potluck. The beef-and-bean filling, cheese and crunchy chips have mass appeal.
—**ANITA WILSON** MANSFIELD, OH

PREP: 1 HOUR • **BAKE:** 20 MIN.
MAKES: 2 CASSEROLES
(15 SERVINGS EACH)

- 2   pounds ground beef
- 2   large onions, chopped
- 2   large green peppers, chopped
- 2   cans (28 ounces each) diced tomatoes, undrained
- 2   cans (16 ounces each) hot chili beans, undrained
- 2   cans (15 ounces each) black beans, rinsed and drained
- 2   cans (11 ounces each) whole kernel corn, drained
- 2   cans (8 ounces each) tomato sauce
- 2   envelopes taco seasoning
- 2   packages (13 ounces each) spicy nacho-flavored tortilla chips
- 4   cups (16 ounces) shredded cheddar cheese

1. In a Dutch oven, cook the beef, onions and green peppers over medium heat until the meat is no longer pink, breaking the meat into crumbles; drain. Stir in the tomatoes, beans, corn, tomato sauce and taco seasoning. Bring to a boil. Reduce heat; simmer, uncovered, for 30 minutes (mixture will be thin).

2. In each of two greased 13x9-in. baking dishes, layer 5 cups of chips and $4\frac{2}{3}$ cups of meat mixture. Repeat layers. Top each with 4 cups of chips and 2 cups of cheese.

3. Bake the casseroles, uncovered, at 350° for 20-25 minutes or until golden brown.

DID YOU KNOW?

While green peppers and other peppers are commonly referred to as vegetables, they are technically classified as fruits. Other favorites that are treated as veggies but are actually fruits include tomatoes, beans, cucumbers, squash, peapods and avocadoes.

POTLUCK

Best Shepherd's Pie

I received this economical pie recipe from a friend who was a wiz at pinching pennies without sacrificing flavor. Try it and see!

—**VALERIE MERRILL** TOPEKA, KS

PREP: 20 MIN. • **BAKE:** 30 MIN.
MAKES: 8-10 SERVINGS

$2\frac{1}{2}$ pounds potatoes, peeled and cooked
  1 to $1\frac{1}{2}$ cups (8 to 12 ounces) sour cream
      Salt and pepper to taste
  2 pounds ground beef
$\frac{1}{2}$ cup chopped onion
  1 medium sweet red pepper, chopped
  1 teaspoon garlic salt
  1 can ($10\frac{3}{4}$ ounces) condensed cream of mushroom soup, undiluted
  1 can (16 ounces) whole kernel corn, drained
$\frac{1}{2}$ cup milk
  2 tablespoons butter, melted
      Chopped fresh parsley, optional

1. In a large bowl, mash potatoes with sour cream. Add salt and pepper; set aside. In a large skillet, cook beef with onion and red pepper until meat is no longer pink and vegetables are tender; drain. Stir garlic salt into meat mixture. Stir in the soup, corn and milk.

2. Spread meat mixture into a 13x9-in. baking dish. Top with mashed potatoes; drizzle with butter.

3. Bake the pie, uncovered, at 350° for 30-35 minutes or until heated through. For additional browning, place under broiler for a few minutes. Sprinkle with parsley if desired.

TOP TIP

For the fluffiest mashed potatoes, use only russet potatoes. Cook them just until tender; immediately drain them and let them stand uncovered for 1-2 minutes before mashing.

Short Rib Cobbler

Stew and biscuits are favorites in our family, so I tried combining the two like a cobbler. Golden brown from the oven, this supper's about as down-home as it gets.

—JANINE TALLEY ORLANDO, FL

PREP: 45 MIN. • **BAKE:** 3 HOURS
MAKES: 8 SERVINGS

- ½ cup plus 3 tablespoons all-purpose flour, divided
- 1¼ teaspoons salt, divided
- ½ teaspoon pepper
- 2 pounds well-trimmed boneless beef short ribs, cut into 1½-in. pieces
- 5 tablespoons olive oil, divided
- 1 large onion, chopped
- 1 medium carrot, chopped
- 1 celery rib, chopped
- 1 garlic clove, minced
- 2 tablespoons tomato paste
- 5 cups beef stock
- 1 cup dry red wine or additional beef stock
- 1 teaspoon poultry seasoning
- 1 bay leaf
- 1 package (14 ounces) frozen pearl onions, thawed
- 4 medium carrots, cut into 2-inch pieces

COBBLER TOPPING

- 2 cups biscuit/baking mix
- ⅔ cup 2% milk
  Fresh thyme leaves

1. Preheat oven to 350°. In a shallow bowl, mix ½ cup flour, ¾ teaspoon salt and pepper. Dip the short ribs in flour mixture to coat all sides; shake off excess.

2. In an ovenproof Dutch oven, heat 3 tablespoons olive oil over medium heat. Brown beef in batches. Remove from pan.

3. In the same pan, heat the remaining oil over medium heat. Add the onion, chopped carrot and celery; cook and stir 2-3 minutes or until tender. Add garlic; cook 1 minute longer. Stir in the tomato paste and remaining flour until blended. Gradually stir in the beef stock and wine until smooth. Return beef to pan; stir in poultry seasoning, bay leaf and remaining salt. Bring to a boil.

4. Bake, covered, 1¾ hours. Stir in pearl onions and carrot pieces. Bake, covered, 30-45 minutes longer or until the beef and onions are tender. Skim fat and remove bay leaf.

5. In a small bowl, mix biscuit mix and milk just until a soft dough forms. Drop by scant ¼ cupfuls over beef mixture. Bake, uncovered, 40-45 minutes longer or until topping is golden brown. Sprinkle with thyme.

**Easy Cheddar
Chicken Potpie, p. 100**

CHAPTER 4

CHICKEN & TURKEY

Turn to these classics when you crave a one-dish sensation.

Creamy Buffalo Chicken Enchiladas

I'm big on spicy food, but not everyone shares my passion. Luckily, a creamy three-ingredient topping makes these enchiladas easy for everyone to love.

—CRYSTAL SCHLUETER NORTHGLENN, CO

PREP: 15 MIN. • **BAKE:** 25 MIN.
MAKES: 6 SERVINGS

3 cups shredded rotisserie chicken
1 can (10 ounces) enchilada sauce
¼ cup Buffalo wing sauce
1¼ cups (5 ounces) shredded Monterey Jack or cheddar cheese, divided
12 corn tortillas (6 inches), warmed
1 can (10¾ ounces) condensed cream of celery soup, undiluted
½ cup blue cheese salad dressing
¼ cup 2% milk
¼ teaspoon chili powder
 Optional toppings: sour cream, thinly sliced green onions and additional Buffalo wing sauce

1. Preheat oven to 350°. In a large bowl, mix chicken, enchilada sauce and wing sauce. Stir in ¾ cup cheese.

2. Place ¼ cup chicken mixture off center on each tortilla. Roll up and place in a greased 13x9-in. baking dish, seam side down.

3. In a small bowl, mix the soup, salad dressing and milk; pour over enchiladas. Sprinkle with remaining cheese; top with chili powder.

4. Bake, uncovered, 25-30 minutes or until heated through and cheese is melted. Add toppings as desired.

FREEZE OPTION Cover and freeze unbaked casserole. To use, partially thaw in refrigerator overnight. Remove from refrigerator 30 minutes before baking. Preheat oven to 350°. Bake casserole as directed, increasing time as necessary to heat through and for a thermometer inserted in center to read 165°.

Chicken Taco Pie

This family fave comes to the rescue on busy nights when we've been rushing to soccer, swimming lessons or Scouts. I make it in the morning and just pop it in the oven when we arrive home.

—KAREN LATIMER WINNIPEG, MB

PREP: 20 MIN. • **BAKE:** 30 MIN.
MAKES: 6 SERVINGS

- 1 tube (8 ounces) refrigerated crescent rolls
- 1 pound ground chicken
- 1 envelope taco seasoning
- 1 can (4 ounces) chopped green chilies
- ½ cup water
- ½ cup salsa
- ½ cup shredded Mexican cheese blend
- 1 cup shredded lettuce
- 1 small sweet red pepper, chopped
- 1 small green pepper, chopped
- 1 medium tomato, seeded and chopped
- 1 green onion, thinly sliced
- 2 tablespoons pickled jalapeno slices
  Sour cream and additional salsa

1. Preheat oven to 350°. Unroll crescent dough and separate into triangles. Press onto bottom of a greased 9-in. pie plate to form a crust, sealing seams well. Bake 18-20 minutes or until golden brown.

2. In a large skillet, cook chicken over medium heat 6-8 minutes or until no longer pink, breaking into crumbles; drain. Stir in taco seasoning, green chilies, water and salsa; bring to a boil.

3. Spoon into crust; sprinkle with cheese. Bake 8-10 minutes or until cheese is melted.

4. Top with lettuce, peppers, tomato, green onion and pickled jalapeno. Serve with sour cream and additional salsa.

TOP TIP

Chicken Taco Pie is a complete meal-in-one but feel free to get creative when rounding out a menu. For instance, serve the savory entree alongside bowls of cheese soup or even chili. Microwave canned refried beans, prepare Spanish rice from a mix or simply open a bag of tortilla chips and a jar of salsa.

POTLUCK

Stuffing & Turkey Casserole

This is a plate full of love, comfort and goodness. Give it a try and you'll instantly understand what I mean!

—DEBBIE FABRE FORT MYERS, FL

PREP: 15 MIN. • **BAKE:** 45 MIN. + STANDING
MAKES: 12 SERVINGS

4	cups leftover stuffing
1	cup dried cranberries
1	cup chopped pecans
¾	cup chicken broth
1	egg, lightly beaten
2	cups (8 ounces) shredded part-skim mozzarella cheese
1	cup whole-milk ricotta cheese
4	cups cubed cooked turkey, divided
1	cup (4 ounces) shredded cheddar cheese

1. Preheat oven to 350°. Place stuffing, cranberries and pecans in a large bowl; stir in broth. In a small bowl, mix egg and mozzarella and ricotta cheeses.

2. In a greased 13x9-in. baking dish, layer 2 cups turkey, 3 cups stuffing mixture and ricotta cheese mixture. Top with remaining turkey and stuffing mixture. Sprinkle with cheddar cheese.

3. Bake, covered, 40-45 minutes or until heated through. Bake, uncovered, 5 minutes longer. Let stand 10 minutes before serving.

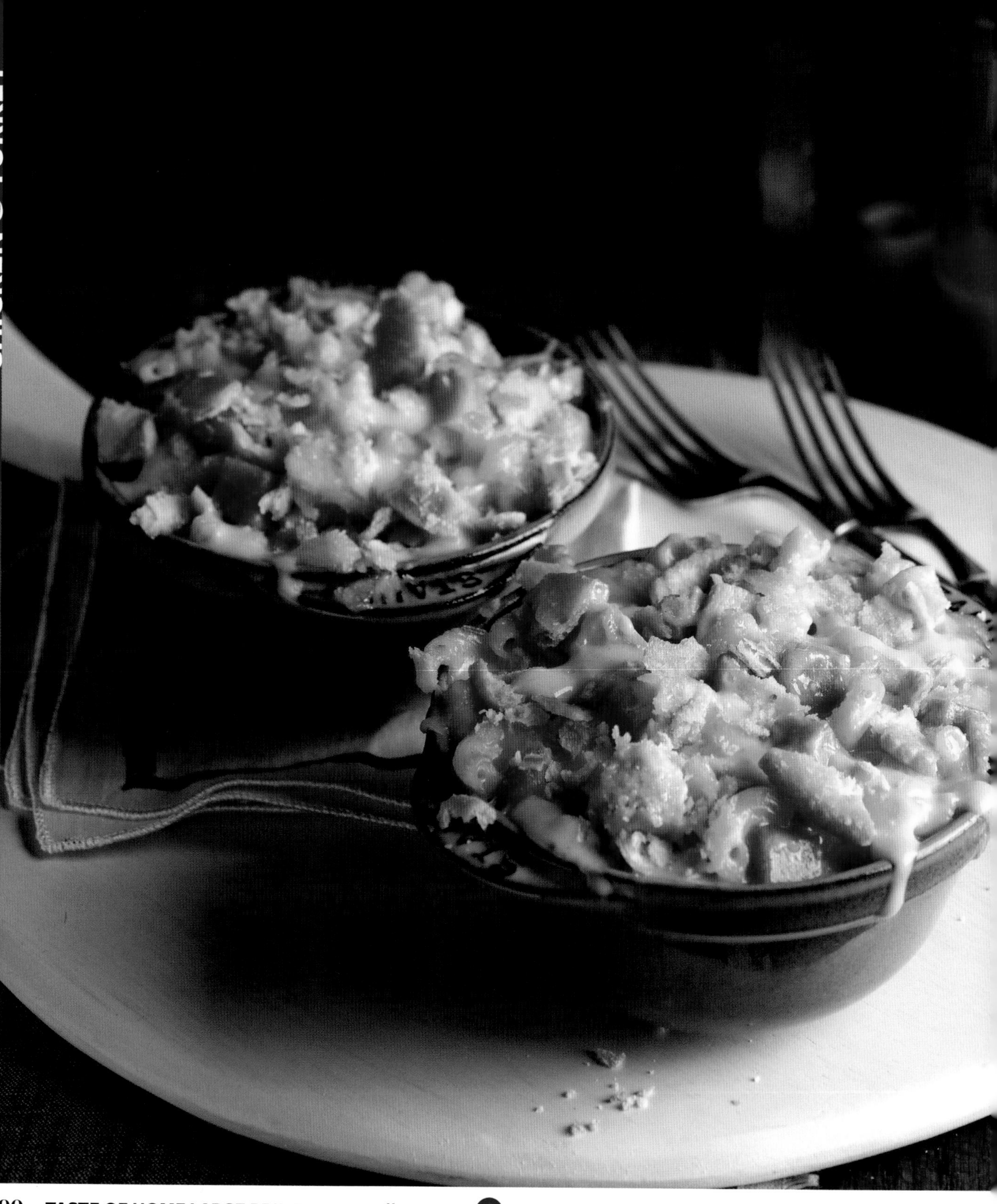

Turkey Cordon Bleu Casserole

We love the flavors of traditional cordon bleu, and this variation is so easy to make. It's a delicious way to use up leftover cooked ham and turkey.

—KRISTINE BLAUERT WABASHA, MN

PREP: 20 MIN. • **BAKE:** 25 MIN.
MAKES: 8 SERVINGS

- 2 cups uncooked elbow macaroni
- 2 cans (10¾ ounces each) condensed cream of chicken soup, undiluted
- ¾ cup 2% milk
- ¼ cup grated Parmesan cheese
- 1 teaspoon prepared mustard
- 1 teaspoon paprika
- ½ teaspoon dried rosemary, crushed
- ¼ teaspoon garlic powder
- ⅛ teaspoon rubbed sage
- 2 cups cubed cooked turkey
- 2 cups cubed fully cooked ham
- 2 cups (8 ounces) shredded part-skim mozzarella cheese
- ¼ cup crushed Ritz crackers

1. Preheat oven to 350°. Cook macaroni according to package directions.

2. Meanwhile, in a large bowl, whisk soup, milk, Parmesan cheese, mustard and seasonings. Stir in turkey, ham and mozzarella cheese.

3. Drain macaroni; add to soup mixture and toss to combine. Transfer to eight greased 8-oz. ramekins. Sprinkle with crushed crackers. Bake, uncovered, 25-30 minutes or until bubbly.

FREEZE OPTION Cover and freeze unbaked casserole. To use, partially thaw in refrigerator overnight. Remove from refrigerator 30 minutes before baking. Preheat oven to 350°. Bake as directed, increasing time as necessary to heat through and for a thermometer inserted in center to read 165°.

Turkey Alfredo Tetrazzini

Jarred Alfredo sauce, canned mushrooms and onion powder put a fast spin on my mother-in-law's original tetrazzini recipe. We loved the pop of color from the peas, the hint of white wine and the tangy flavor.

—**JUDY BATSON** TAMPA, FL

PREP: 20 MIN. • **BAKE:** 30 MIN.
MAKES: 4 SERVINGS

- 4 ounces thin spaghetti
- 1 jar (15 ounces) Alfredo sauce
- 2 cups frozen peas
- 1½ cups cubed cooked turkey or chicken
- 1 can (4 ounces) mushroom stems and pieces, drained
- ¼ cup shredded Swiss cheese
- ¼ cup shredded Parmesan cheese
- 2 tablespoons white wine or chicken broth
- ½ teaspoon onion powder
- ½ cup French-fried onions
- ½ teaspoon paprika

1. Cook spaghetti according to package directions. Meanwhile, in a large bowl, combine the Alfredo sauce, peas, turkey, mushrooms, cheeses, wine and onion powder. Drain spaghetti. Add to sauce mixture; toss to coat. Transfer to a greased 8-in.-square baking dish. Sprinkle with onions and paprika.

2. Cover and bake at 350° for 30-35 minutes or until heated through.

TOP TIP

Garlic and onion powders tend to absorb moisture from the air, especially during warm weather months. Store them in airtight spice jars to keep them as free from moisture and humidity as possible.

Chicken Rice Dinner

Everyone enjoys the country-style combo of chicken, rice and mushrooms. Bouillon adds to the wonderful flavor of this dish.
—**JUDITH ANGLEN** RIVERTON, WY

PREP: 20 MIN. • **BAKE:** 1 HOUR
MAKES: 5 SERVINGS

½ cup all-purpose flour
1 teaspoon salt
½ teaspoon pepper
10 bone-in chicken thighs (about 3¾ pounds)
3 tablespoons canola oil
1 cup uncooked long grain rice
¼ cup chopped onion
2 garlic cloves, minced
1 can (4 ounces) mushroom stems and pieces, undrained
2 teaspoons chicken bouillon granules
2 cups boiling water
Minced fresh parsley, optional

1. In a large resealable plastic bag, combine the flour, salt and pepper. Add chicken thighs, one at a time, and shake to coat. In a large skillet over medium heat, brown chicken in oil.

2. Place the rice in an ungreased 13x9-in. baking dish. Sprinkle with the onion and garlic; top with mushrooms. Dissolve chicken bouillon in boiling water; pour over all. Place chicken on top.

3. Cover; bake at 350° for 1 hour or until a thermometer reads 180° and the rice is tender. Sprinkle with parsley if desired.

Chicken Amandine

With colorful green beans and bright red pimientos, this attractive chicken casserole is terrific for the holidays. It's truly comfort food at its finest.

—**KAT WOOLBRIGHT** WICHITA FALLS, TX

PREP: 35 MIN. • **BAKE:** 30 MIN.
MAKES: 8 SERVINGS

- 1/4 cup chopped onion
- 1 tablespoon butter
- 1 package (6 ounces) long grain and wild rice
- 2 1/4 cups chicken broth
- 3 cups cubed cooked chicken
- 2 cups frozen French-style green beans, thawed
- 1 can (10 3/4 ounces) condensed cream of chicken soup, undiluted
- 3/4 cup sliced almonds, divided
- 1 jar (4 ounces) diced pimientos, drained
- 1 teaspoon pepper
- 1/2 teaspoon garlic powder
- 1 bacon strip, cooked and crumbled

1. In a large saucepan, saute onion in butter until tender. Add rice with contents of seasoning packet and broth. Bring to a boil. Reduce heat; cover and simmer for 25 minutes or until liquid is absorbed. Uncover; set aside to cool.

2. In a large bowl, combine the chicken, green beans, soup, 1/2 cup of almonds, pimientos, pepper and garlic powder. Stir in rice.

3. Transfer to a greased 2 1/2-qt. baking dish. Sprinkle with bacon and remaining almonds. Cover and bake at 350° for 30-35 minutes or until heated through.

TOP TIP

If you like chicken casseroles, keep an eye out for boneless skinless chicken breasts on sale. Bake the chicken, cube the meat and freeze it in measured 1-cup portions. The cooked chicken cubes are wonderful time savers when assembling casseroles or even for use in soups, stews, tacos and other favorites.

Chicken Cheese Lasagna

I like to make a double batch of this lasagna and freeze one for another day. The filling can also be stuffed into manicotti shells.
—**MARY ANN KOSMAS** MINNEAPOLIS, MN

PREP: 25 MIN. • **BAKE:** 35 MIN. + STANDING
MAKES: 12 SERVINGS

- 1   medium onion, chopped
- 1/2 cup butter, cubed
- 1   garlic clove, minced
- 1/2 cup all-purpose flour
- 1   teaspoon salt
- 2   cups chicken broth
- 1 1/2 cups 2% milk
- 4   cups (16 ounces) shredded part-skim mozzarella cheese, divided
- 1   cup grated Parmesan cheese, divided
- 1   teaspoon dried basil
- 1   teaspoon dried oregano
- 1/2 teaspoon white pepper
- 2   cups (15 to 16 ounces) ricotta cheese
- 1   tablespoon minced fresh parsley
- 9   lasagna noodles, cooked and drained
- 2   packages (10 ounces each) frozen spinach, thawed and well drained
- 2   cups cubed cooked chicken

1. In a large saucepan, saute onion in butter until tender. Add garlic; cook 1 minute longer. Stir in flour and salt until blended; cook until bubbly. Gradually stir in broth and milk. Bring to a boil; cook and stir for 1 minute or until thickened. Stir in 2 cups mozzarella cheese, 1/2 cup Parmesan cheese, basil, oregano and pepper; set aside.

2. In a large bowl, combine the ricotta cheese, parsley and the remaining mozzarella; set aside. Spread one-fourth of the cheese sauce into a greased 13x9-in. baking dish; cover with one-third of the noodles. Layer with half of the ricotta mixture, half of the spinach and half of the chicken.

3. Cover with one-fourth of the cheese sauce and one-third of the noodles. Repeat layers of the ricotta mixture, spinach, chicken and one-fourth cheese sauce. Cover with remaining noodles and cheese sauce.

4. Sprinkle with remaining Parmesan cheese. Bake at 350°, uncovered, for 35-40 minutes. Let stand 15 minutes.

NOTE For a change, substitute cooked bulk Italian sausage for the chicken. You can also use no-cook lasagna noodles without making adjustments to the liquid or cooking time.

Easy Cheddar Chicken Potpie

My kids love chicken potpie, and I really like that this is so quick and easy to put together with frozen veggies and store-bought gravy. To make it even simpler, my friend and I decided to top it with a biscuit crust instead of homemade pastry. It's delicious!

—LINDA DREES PALESTINE, TX

PREP: 20 MIN. • **BAKE:** 25 MIN.
MAKES: 6 SERVINGS

- 1 package (16 ounces) frozen vegetables for stew, thawed and coarsely chopped
- 1 jar (12 ounces) chicken gravy
- 2 cups (8 ounces) shredded cheddar cheese
- 2 cups cubed cooked chicken
- 1 cup biscuit/baking mix
- 1/4 teaspoon dried thyme
- 2 eggs
- 1/4 cup 2% milk

1. Combine vegetables and gravy in a large saucepan. Bring to a boil. Reduce heat; stir in cheese and chicken. Cook and stir until cheese is melted. Pour into a greased 11x7-in. baking dish.

2. Combine biscuit mix and thyme in a small bowl. In another bowl, whisk the eggs and milk; stir into dry ingredients just until moistened. Drop by tablespoonfuls over chicken mixture; spread gently.

3. Bake, uncovered, at 375° for 23-27 minutes or until golden brown. Let stand for 5 minutes before serving.

Cajun Chicken Fettuccine

I combined two pasta sauces and added Cajun seasoning for a little kick in this quick-to-fix casserole. Using frozen onions and peppers speeds things up even more. Try adding mushrooms or frozen peas.
—**REBECCA REECE** HENDERSON, NV

PREP: 25 MIN. • **BAKE:** 25 MIN.
MAKES: 8 SERVINGS

- 8   ounces uncooked fettuccine
- 1   large sweet onion, halved and sliced
- 1   medium green pepper, cut into ¼-inch strips
- 1   medium sweet red pepper, cut into ¼-inch strips
- 2   tablespoons olive oil
- 2   cups cubed cooked chicken
- 4   teaspoons Cajun seasoning
- 1   teaspoon minced garlic
- 1   jar (15 ounces) Alfredo sauce
- ½   cup spaghetti sauce
- 2   cups (8 ounces) shredded part-skim mozzarella cheese
- ½   cup grated Parmesan cheese

1. Cook fettuccine according to package directions. Meanwhile, in a large skillet, saute onion and peppers in oil until tender. Add chicken, Cajun seasoning and garlic; heat through. Transfer to a large bowl. Drain fettuccine; add to chicken mixture. Stir in Alfredo and spaghetti sauces.

2. Transfer to a greased 13x9-in. baking dish. Sprinkle with cheeses. Cover and bake at 375° for 15 minutes. Uncover; bake 10-15 minutes longer or until golden brown.

3. Serve immediately or before baking, cover and freeze casserole for up to 3 months.

TO USE FROZEN CASSEROLE Remove from the freezer 30 minutes before baking (do not thaw). Cover and bake at 350° for 70 minutes. Uncover; bake 5-10 minutes longer or until heated through. Let stand for 10 minutes before serving.

Pan-Roasted Chicken and Vegetables

This one-dish meal tastes like it needs hours of hands-on time to put together, but it takes just minutes to prep the simple ingredients.

—SHERRI MELOTIK OAK CREEK, WI

PREP: 15 MIN. • **BAKE:** 45 MIN.
MAKES: 6 SERVINGS

- 2 pounds red potatoes (about 6 medium), cut into ¾-inch pieces
- 1 large onion, coarsely chopped
- 2 tablespoons olive oil
- 3 garlic cloves, minced
- 1¼ teaspoons salt, divided
- 1 teaspoon dried rosemary, crushed, divided
- ¾ teaspoon pepper, divided
- ½ teaspoon paprika
- 6 bone-in chicken thighs (about 2¼ pounds), skin removed
- 6 cups fresh baby spinach (about 6 ounces)

1. Preheat oven to 425°. In a large bowl, combine potatoes, onion, oil, garlic, ¾ teaspoon salt, ½ teaspoon rosemary and ½ teaspoon pepper; toss to coat. Transfer to a 15x10-in. baking pan coated with cooking spray.

2. In a small bowl, mix paprika and the remaining salt, rosemary and pepper. Sprinkle chicken with paprika mixture; arrange over the vegetables. Roast 35-40 minutes or until a thermometer inserted in chicken reads 170°-175° and vegetables are just tender.

3. Remove chicken to a serving platter; keep warm. Top vegetables with spinach. Roast 8-10 minutes longer or until the vegetables are tender and the spinach is wilted. Stir vegetables to combine; serve with the chicken.

Spinach Chicken Casserole

I created this dish based on a recipe I found on a spaghetti sauce label. I made a few substitutions and additions and was quite pleased with the results.

—JACKIE WOOD JACKSON, TN

PREP: 20 MIN. • **BAKE:** 20 MIN.
MAKES: 6 SERVINGS

- 2 cups uncooked penne pasta
- ¾ pound boneless skinless chicken breasts, cubed
- 1 small onion, chopped
- ½ cup chopped green pepper
- 1 jar (26 ounces) spaghetti sauce
- 1 package (16 ounces) frozen leaf spinach, thawed and squeezed dry
- 1 jar (6 ounces) sliced mushrooms, drained
- 1 can (2¼ ounces) sliced ripe olives, drained
- 2 cups (8 ounces) shredded part-skim mozzarella cheese, divided

1. Cook pasta according to package directions. Meanwhile, in a large nonstick saucepan coated with cooking spray, saute chicken until no longer pink; set aside.

2. In the same pan, saute the onion and green pepper until crisp-tender. Add spaghetti sauce, spinach, mushrooms and ripe olives. Bring to a boil. Reduce the heat; simmer, uncovered, for 5 minutes. Drain the pasta; add the chicken and pasta to pan. Sprinkle with 1 cup mozzarella cheese and toss to coat.

3. Transfer to a 13x9-in. baking dish coated with cooking spray; sprinkle with remaining cheese. Cover and bake at 350° for 20-25 minutes or until cheese is melted.

Roasted Kielbasa &
Vegetables, p. 121

CHAPTER 5

PORK, SAUSAGE & HAM

Turn here for savory dinners sure to become new favorites.

Scalloped Potatoes & Ham Casserole

I'm a home health nurse and received this recipe from one of my elderly clients, who had used it for years. Now, it's one of my family's favorites. It will never curdle, thanks to the secret ingredient of powdered nondairy creamer.

—KATHY JOHNSON LAKE CITY, SD

PREP: 25 MIN. • **BAKE:** 1 HOUR
MAKES: 6 SERVINGS

- ¾ cup powdered nondairy creamer
- 1¾ cups water
- 3 tablespoons butter
- 3 tablespoons all-purpose flour
- 2 tablespoons dried minced onion
- 1 teaspoon salt
- ¾ teaspoon paprika
- 6 large potatoes, peeled and thinly sliced
- 2 cups diced fully cooked ham
- 1 cup (4 ounces) shredded cheddar cheese

1. Preheat oven to 350°. In a small bowl, mix creamer and water until smooth. In a small saucepan, heat butter over medium heat. Stir in flour, onion, salt and paprika until smooth; gradually add creamer mixture. Bring to a boil; cook and stir 1-2 minutes or until thickened.

2. In a greased 13x9-in. baking dish, layer potatoes and ham; pour sauce over top. Bake, covered, 15 minutes. Uncover; bake 40-50 minutes longer or until potatoes are tender. Sprinkle with cheese; bake 5-10 minutes or until edges are bubbly and cheese is melted.

TOP TIP

It's important to preheat your oven before baking a casserole. Baked items depend on the correct oven temperature to help them rise and cook properly. Always place the oven racks at the proper levels first, then set the temperature stated in the recipe. All *Taste of Home* recipes are tested in preheated ovens.

Italian Sausage Rigatoni Bake

This casserole combines all of our favorite Italian flavors, but the fresh mozzarella really sets it apart from other recipes.

—**BLAIR LONERGAN** ROCHELLE, VA

PREP: 30 MIN. • **BAKE:** 25 MIN.
MAKES: 2 CASSEROLES
(4 SERVINGS EACH)

---

1 package (16 ounces) rigatoni
1 pound bulk Italian sausage
8 ounces sliced fresh mushrooms
1 medium sweet red pepper, chopped
5 cups marinara sauce
1/4 cup grated Parmesan cheese
2 tablespoons half-and-half cream
16 ounces sliced part-skim mozzarella cheese

1. Preheat oven to 375°. Cook rigatoni according to package directions; drain.

2. In a large skillet, cook the sausage, mushrooms and pepper over medium-high heat 8-10 minutes or until sausage is no longer pink and vegetables are tender, breaking up sausage into crumbles; drain. Stir in marinara sauce, Parmesan cheese and cream. Add rigatoni and toss to coat.

3. In each of two greased 8-in.-square baking dishes, layer one-fourth of the rigatoni mixture and one-fourth of the mozzarella cheese. Repeat layers. Bake, uncovered, 25-35 minutes or until heated through and cheese is melted. (Cover loosely with foil if top browns too quickly.)

FREEZE OPTION Cool unbaked casseroles; cover and freeze. To use, partially thaw in refrigerator overnight. Remove from refrigerator 30 minutes before baking. Preheat oven to 375°. Bake casseroles as directed, increasing time as necessary to heat through and for a thermometer inserted in the center to read 165°.

TOP TIP

Preparing Italian Sausage Rigatoni Bake for a group? Simply swap out the two 8-in.-square baking dishes for one 13x9-in. baking dish. Follow recipe as directed, using the one baking pan. Bake as directed, increasing the cooking time as needed to heat through and for a thermometer to read 165°.

Sauerkraut Hot Dish

We often serve this hearty entree at family gatherings, and the men especially seem to enjoy it. My sister gave me this recipe about 15 years ago, and it has been a favorite ever since. The blend of ingredients is a pleasant surprise.

—**NEDRA PARKER** DUNBAR, WI

PREP: 15 MIN. • **BAKE:** 1½ HOURS
MAKES: 6-8 SERVINGS

1½ pounds pork stew meat
1 medium onion, chopped
2 celery ribs, chopped
1 can (14 ounces) sauerkraut, undrained
8 ounces egg noodles, cooked and drained
1 can (10¾ ounces) condensed cream of mushroom soup, undiluted
1 jar (4½ ounces) whole mushrooms, drained
Salt and pepper to taste

1. In a skillet, cook pork over medium heat until no longer pink. Add the onion and celery; cook until vegetables are crisp-tender. Stir in the sauerkraut, noodles, soup and mushrooms; sprinkle with salt and pepper.

2. Spoon into a greased 2-qt. baking dish. Cover and bake at 350° for 1½ hours or until the meat is tender, stirring occasionally.

Sausage Lasagna Rolls

Who said lasagna noodles have to lie flat?
This creation is what we call a "casser-roll."
—**KALI WRASPIR** OLYMPIA, WA

PREP: 45 MIN. • **BAKE:** 45 MIN.
MAKES: 2 CASSEROLES
(6 SERVINGS EACH)

- 12 lasagna noodles
- 1 pound bulk Italian sausage
- 2 jars (26 ounces each) spaghetti sauce
- 1 carton (15 ounces) ricotta cheese
- 2 cups (8 ounces) shredded part-skim mozzarella cheese, divided
- ¾ cup shredded Parmesan cheese, divided
- 1 egg
- 2 tablespoons minced fresh parsley or 2 teaspoons dried parsley flakes
- 2½ teaspoons minced fresh rosemary or ¾ teaspoon dried rosemary, crushed
- 2 teaspoons lemon juice
- 1½ teaspoons minced fresh thyme or ½ teaspoon dried thyme
- 1 teaspoon grated lemon peel
- 1 teaspoon coarsely ground pepper
- ½ teaspoon salt

1. Preheat oven to 350°. Cook noodles according to package directions Meanwhile, in a large skillet, cook the sausage over medium heat until no longer pink; drain. Stir in spaghetti sauce.

2. In a large bowl, combine ricotta, 1 cup mozzarella, ¼ cup Parmesan, egg, parsley, rosemary, lemon juice, thyme, lemon peel, pepper and salt. Drain noodles. Spread 2 tablespoons cheese mixture on each noodle; carefully roll up.

3. Spread ⅔ cup meat sauce into each of two greased 11x7-in. baking dishes. Place roll-ups seam side down over sauce. Top with remaining meat sauce. Sprinkle with remaining mozzarella and Parmesan cheeses. Cover and bake 45-50 minutes or until bubbly.

FREEZE OPTION Cover and freeze unbaked casseroles up to 3 months. To use, thaw in the refrigerator overnight. Remove from refrigerator 30 minutes before baking. Preheat oven to 350°. Cover and bake 50-60 minutes or until bubbly.

POTLUCK

Creamy Cavatappi & Cheese

Dive fork first into oodles of noodles coated with a to-die-for sharp cheddar cheese sauce in this grown-up mac and cheese. Hot sauce lends a mild heat that's delectable with the smoky topping.

—**BARBARA COLUCCI** ROCKLEDGE, FL

PREP: 30 MIN. • **BAKE:** 20 MIN.
MAKES: 10 SERVINGS

- 6 cups uncooked cavatappi or spiral pasta
- 3 garlic cloves, minced
- 1/3 cup butter
- 1/4 cup all-purpose flour
- 1 tablespoon hot pepper sauce
- 4 cups 2% milk
- 6 cups (24 ounces) shredded sharp cheddar cheese
- 1 cup cubed process cheese (Velveeta)
- 3 green onions, chopped

TOPPINGS
- 1/2 cup panko (Japanese) bread crumbs
- 3 thick-sliced bacon strips, cooked and coarsley crumbled
- 1 tablespoon butter, melted
- 1 green onion, chopped
  Coarsely ground pepper, optional

1. Cook cavatappi according to package directions.

2. Meanwhile, saute garlic in butter in a Dutch oven. Stir in flour and pepper sauce until blended; gradually add milk. Bring to a boil; cook and stir for 2 minutes or until thickened.

3. Stir in cheeses until melted; add green onions. Drain cavatappi; stir into cheese mixture.

4. Transfer to a greased 13x9-in. baking dish. Combine the bread crumbs, bacon and melted butter; sprinkle over top.

5. Bake, uncovered, at 350° for 20-25 minutes or until bubbly. Sprinkle with green onion and, if desired, pepper.

TOP TIP

Not only are mac-and-cheese casseroles ideal contributions to charity potlucks, family reunions and other events, but their versatility is amazing. Toss in some cooked and cubed ham or chicken, sauteed mushroom and onions, frozen peas, chopped peppers or even imitation lobster. Get creative! The possibilities are endless.

Roasted Kielbasa & Vegetables

What's the number one reason I like kielbasa with vegetables? It's a healthy yet tasty approach to dinner!
—**MARIETTA SLATER** JUSTIN, TX

PREP: 20 MIN. • **BAKE:** 40 MIN.
MAKES: 6 SERVINGS

- 3 medium sweet potatoes, peeled and cut into 1-inch pieces
- 1 large sweet onion, cut into 1-inch pieces
- 4 medium carrots, cut into 1-inch pieces
- 2 tablespoons olive oil
- 1 pound smoked kielbasa or Polish sausage, halved and cut into 1-inch pieces
- 1 medium yellow summer squash, cut into 1-inch pieces
- 1 medium zucchini, cut into 1-inch pieces
- ¼ teaspoon salt
- ¼ teaspoon pepper
  Dijon mustard, optional

1. Preheat oven to 400°. Divide the sweet potatoes, onion and carrots between two greased 15x10-in. baking pans. Drizzle with oil; toss to coat. Roast 25 minutes, stirring occasionally.

2. Add the kielbasa, squash and zucchini to pans; sprinkle with salt and pepper. Roast 15-20 minutes longer or until vegetables are tender. Transfer to a serving bowl; toss to combine. Serve with mustard if desired.

POTLUCK

Hawaiian Pizza Pasta

I discovered this recipe a while ago and have been making it ever since. Over the years, I've tweaked it to suit my family. Feel free to substitute chopped salami, pepperoni or cooked ground beef for the ham. Or, add red peppers, olives—whatever you like on pizzas!

—ROSE ENNS ABBOTSFORD, BC

PREP: 30 MIN. • **BAKE:** 30 MIN.
MAKES: 12 SERVINGS

½ pound sliced fresh mushrooms
1 medium onion, chopped
1 medium green pepper, chopped
3 tablespoons canola oil
2 garlic cloves, minced
1 can (15 ounces) tomato sauce
2 bay leaves
1 teaspoon dried oregano
1 teaspoon dried basil
½ teaspoon sugar
3½ cups uncooked spiral pasta
6 cups (24 ounces) shredded part-skim mozzarella cheese, divided
1 can (20 ounces) pineapple chunks, drained
1 cup cubed fully cooked ham

1. In a large saucepan, saute the mushrooms, onion and pepper in oil for 5 minutes or until tender. Add garlic; cook 1 minute longer. Add the tomato sauce, bay leaves, oregano, basil and sugar. Bring to a boil. Reduce heat; simmer, uncovered, for 20-30 minutes or until thickened, stirring frequently.

2. Meanwhile, cook pasta according to package directions; drain. Discard bay leaves from sauce. Stir in the pasta, 5 cups of mozzarella cheese, pineapple and ham.

3. Transfer to a greased shallow 3-qt. baking dish. Sprinkle with remaining cheese. Bake, uncovered, at 350° for 30-35 minutes or until heated through.

TOP TIP

When recipes call for cup measurements of chopped veggies, remember that a medium green pepper, chopped, will yield about 1 cup. A large green pepper, chopped, will yield about 1⅓ to 1½ cups. A medium onion, chopped, will equal about ½ cup; a large onion will yield about 1 cup.

Pan Roasted Pork Chops & Potatoes

A shortcut marinade gives these pork chops plenty of flavor, and the crumb coating packs on the crunch. For color, I like to add a few handfuls of Brussels sprouts to the tasty one-dish meal.

—CHAR OUELLETTE COLTON, OR

PREP: 20 MIN. + MARINATING
BAKE: 40 MIN. • **MAKES:** 4 SERVINGS

- 4 boneless pork loin chops (6 ounces each)
- ½ cup plus 2 tablespoons reduced-fat Italian salad dressing, divided
- 4 small potatoes (about 1½ pounds)
- ½ pound fresh Brussels sprouts, trimmed and halved
- ½ cup soft bread crumbs
- 1 tablespoon minced fresh parsley
- ¼ teaspoon salt
- ⅛ teaspoon pepper
- 2 teaspoons butter, melted

1. Place pork chops and ½ cup salad dressing in a large resealable plastic bag; seal bag and turn to coat. Refrigerate 8 hours or overnight. Cover and refrigerate remaining salad dressing.

2. Preheat oven to 400°. Cut each potato lengthwise into 12 wedges. Arrange potatoes and Brussels sprouts on a 15x10-in. baking pan coated with cooking spray. Drizzle vegetables with remaining salad dressing; toss to coat. Roast 20 minutes.

3. Drain pork, discarding marinade. Pat pork dry with paper towel. Stir vegetables; place pork chops over top. Roast 15-20 minutes longer or until a thermometer inserted in pork reads 145°. Preheat broiler.

4. In a small bowl, combine bread crumbs, parsley, salt and pepper; stir in butter. Top pork with crumb mixture. Broil 4-6 in. from heat 1-2 minutes or until bread crumbs are golden brown. Let stand 5 minutes.

NOTE To make soft bread crumbs, tear bread into pieces and place in a food processor or blender. Cover and pulse until crumbs form. One slice of bread yields ½ to ¾ cup crumbs.

Ham & Swiss Casserole

When I prepare this noodle casserole for church gatherings, it's always a hit. It can easily be doubled or tripled for a crowd.
—**DORIS BARB** EL DORADO, KS

PREP: 15 MIN. • **BAKE:** 40 MIN.
MAKES: 6-8 SERVINGS

- 1   package (8 ounces) egg noodles, cooked and drained
- 2   cups cubed fully cooked ham
- 2   cups (8 ounces) shredded Swiss cheese
- 1   can (10¾ ounces) condensed cream of celery soup, undiluted
- 1   cup (8 ounces) sour cream
- ½   cup chopped green pepper
- ½   cup chopped onion

1. In a greased 13x9-in. baking dish, layer half of the egg noodles, ham and cheese.

2. In a large bowl, combine the soup, sour cream, green pepper and onion; spread half over the top. Repeat layers. Bake, uncovered, at 350° for 40-45 minutes or until heated through.

Bacon Tortellini Bake

I stirred up an easy pasta and figured if we all like it, others might, too. Broccoli and bacon add color and crunch to this creamy dish.
—**AMY LENTS** GRAND FORKS, ND

PREP: 25 MIN. • **BAKE:** 15 MIN.
MAKES: 6 SERVINGS

- 1 package (20 ounces) refrigerated cheese tortellini
- 3 cups small fresh broccoli florets
- 1/2 pound bacon strips, cut into 1-inch pieces
- 2 garlic cloves, minced
- 1 tablespoon all-purpose flour
- 1 teaspoon dried basil
- 1/2 teaspoon salt
- 1/8 teaspoon coarsely ground pepper
- 2 cups 2% milk
- 3/4 cup shredded part-skim mozzarella cheese, divided
- 3/4 cup grated Parmesan cheese, divided
- 2 teaspoons lemon juice

1. Preheat oven to 350°. Cook tortellini according to package directions, adding broccoli during the last 2 minutes; drain.

2. Meanwhile, in a large skillet, cook bacon over medium heat until crisp, stirring occasionally. Remove with a slotted spoon; drain on paper towels. Discard drippings, reserving 1 tablespoon in pan.

3. Reduce heat to medium-low. Add garlic to drippings in pan; cook and stir 1 minute. Stir in flour, basil, salt and pepper until blended; gradually whisk in milk. Bring to a boil, stirring constantly; cook and stir 3-5 minutes or until slightly thickened. Remove from heat.

4. Stir in 1/2 cup mozzarella cheese, 1/2 cup Parmesan cheese and lemon juice. Add tortellini mixture and bacon; toss to combine. Transfer to a greased 13x9-in. baking dish; sprinkle with remaining cheeses. Bake, uncovered, 15-20 minutes or until heated through and broccoli is tender.

FREEZE OPTION Sprinkle remaining cheeses over unbaked casserole. Cover and freeze. To use, partially thaw in refrigerator overnight. Remove from refrigerator 30 minutes before baking. Preheat oven to 350°. Bake casserole as directed, increasing time as necessary to heat through and for a thermometer inserted in center to read 165°.

POTLUCK

Southwestern Potpie with Cornmeal Biscuits

My change-of-pace potpie is ideal for any gathering. The cornmeal gives the biscuits a delightful little crunch.

—**ANDREA BOLDEN** UNIONVILLE, TN

PREP: 35 MIN. + SIMMERING
BAKE: 15 MIN. + STANDING
MAKES: 12 SERVINGS

- ¼ cup all-purpose flour
- 1½ pounds boneless pork loin roast, cut into ½-inch cubes
- 2 tablespoons butter
- 1 jalapeno pepper, seeded and chopped
- 2 garlic cloves, minced
- 2 cups beef broth
- 1 can (14½ ounces) diced tomatoes, undrained
- 1 teaspoon ground cumin
- ½ teaspoon chili powder
- ¼ to ½ teaspoon ground cinnamon
- 1 can (15¼ ounces) whole kernel corn, drained
- 1 can (15 ounces) pinto beans, rinsed and drained
- 1 can (4 ounces) chopped green chilies

BISCUITS
- 3 cups biscuit/baking mix
- ¾ cup cornmeal
- ½ cup shredded cheddar cheese
- 4½ teaspoons sugar
- 1 cup 2% milk

1. Place flour in a resealable plastic bag. Add pork, a few pieces at a time, and shake to coat. In a Dutch oven, brown pork in butter. Remove and set aside.

2. In same pan, saute jalapeno and garlic in drippings 1 minute. Stir in the broth, tomatoes, cumin, chili powder, cinnamon and pork. Bring to a boil. Reduce heat; cover and simmer 1 hour or until pork is tender.

3. Preheat oven to 400°. Add corn, beans and chilies; heat through. Transfer to a greased 13x9-in. baking dish.

4. In a large bowl, combine biscuit mix, cornmeal, cheese and sugar; stir in milk just until moistened. Turn onto a lightly floured surface; knead 8-10 times.

5. Pat or roll out to ½-in. thickness; cut with a floured 2½-in. biscuit cutter. Arrange over meat mixture. Bake 15-18 minutes or until golden brown. Let stand 10 minutes before serving.

NOTE Wear disposable gloves when cutting hot peppers; the oils can burn skin. Avoid touching your face.

Chili Cheese Dog Casserole

If you like corn bread with your chili, this casserole is a must-try.
—*TASTE OF HOME* TEST KITCHEN

PREP: 20 MIN. • **BAKE:** 30 MIN.
MAKES: 6 SERVINGS

- 1 package (8½ ounces) corn bread/muffin mix
- 1 cup chopped green pepper
- ½ cup chopped onion
- ½ cup chopped celery
- 1 tablespoon olive oil
- 1 package (1 pound) hot dogs, halved lengthwise and cut into bite-size pieces
- 1 can (15 ounces) chili with beans
- 2 tablespoons brown sugar
- ½ teaspoon garlic powder
- ½ teaspoon chili powder
- 1 cup (4 ounces) shredded cheddar cheese, divided

1. Prepare corn bread batter according to package directions. Spread half the batter into a greased 8-in.- square baking dish; set aside.

2. In a large skillet, saute the green pepper, onion and celery in oil until crisp-tender. Stir in hot dogs; saute 3-4 minutes longer or until lightly browned. Stir in the chili, brown sugar, garlic powder and chili powder; heat through. Stir in ¾ cup cheese.

3. Spoon over corn bread batter; top with remaining corn bread batter. Sprinkle remaining cheese over the top. Bake, uncovered, at 350° for 28-32 minutes or until a toothpick inserted near the center comes out clean. Let stand for 5 minutes before serving.

Seafood in Tomato
Sauce, p. 151

CHAPTER 6

FISH & SEAFOOD

Switch up your dinner routine with these seafood sensations.

Tater Crust Tuna Pie

I make this pie a lot because it's quick and easy. My husband and I enjoy the combination of mashed potato flakes and french-fried onions in the pastry crust.

—CYNTHIA KOLBERG SYRACUSE, IN

PREP: 15 MIN. • **BAKE:** 30 MIN.
MAKES: 6-8 SERVINGS

CRUST
- 1   cup all-purpose flour
- ½   cup mashed potato flakes
- ½   cup cold butter
- 3   to 4 tablespoons ice water
- 1   can (2.8 ounces) french-fried onions, divided

FILLING
- 1   egg
- 1   can (10¾ ounces) reduced-fat reduced-sodium condensed cream of mushroom soup, undiluted
- 1   cup (4 ounces) shredded cheddar cheese, divided
- ¾   cup mashed potato flakes
- 1   can (6½ ounces) light water-packed tuna, drained and flaked
- 2   tablespoons chopped pimiento-stuffed green olives

1. In a small bowl, combine flour and potato flakes; cut in butter until crumbly. Add water, 1 tablespoon at a time, until dough is moist enough to hold together.

2. Press pastry over bottom and up sides of an ungreased 9-in. pie plate. Flute edge. Set aside ½ cup onions for topping. Sprinkle remaining onions into the pastry shell.

3. In a large bowl, combine the egg, soup, ½ cup cheese, potato flakes, tuna and olives. Spoon into pastry crust.

4. Bake at 350° for 25 minutes or until crust is golden. Sprinkle with remaining cheese and reserved onions; bake 5-10 minutes longer or until cheese is melted. Let stand for 5 minutes before serving.

Mini Scallop Casseroles

Tiny and tender bay scallops take center stage in these miniature dishes. They're reminiscent of potpies, very creamy and packed with flavorful veggies in every bite.
—**VIVIAN MANARY** NEPEAN, ON

PREP: 30 MIN. • **BAKE:** 20 MIN.
MAKES: 4 SERVINGS

- 3 celery ribs, chopped
- 1 cup sliced fresh mushrooms
- 1 medium green pepper, chopped
- 1 small onion, chopped
- 2 tablespoons butter
- 1/3 cup all-purpose flour
- 1/4 teaspoon salt
- 1/4 teaspoon pepper
- 2 cups fat-free milk
- 1 pound bay scallops

TOPPING

- 1 cup soft bread crumbs
- 1 tablespoon butter, melted
- 1/4 cup shredded cheddar cheese

1. In a large skillet, saute the celery, mushrooms, green pepper and onion in butter until tender. Stir in flour, salt and pepper until blended; gradually add milk. Bring to a boil; cook and stir 2 minutes or until thickened.

2. Reduce heat; add the scallops. Cook, stirring occasionally, 3-4 minutes or until scallops are firm and opaque.

3. Preheat oven to 350°. Divide mixture among four 10-oz. ramekins or custard cups. In a small bowl, combine crumbs and butter; sprinkle over scallop mixture.

4. Bake, uncovered, 15-20 minutes or until bubbly. Sprinkle with cheese; bake 5 minutes longer or until cheese is melted.

HOW TO

CHOP AN ONION

❶ To quickly chop an onion, peel and cut it in half from the root to the top, leaving the root attached. Place flat side down on work surface.
❷ Cut vertically through the onion, leaving the root end uncut.
❸ Cut across the onion, discarding the root end. The closer the cuts, the more finely the onion will be chopped.

Baked Orange Roughy and Rice

It might seem hard to believe, but it's true—this delectable fish dinner will dirty just one dish. Your family will be lining up to dig in once they see the beautiful results.

—*TASTE OF HOME* TEST KITCHEN

PREP: 10 MIN. • **BAKE:** 30 MIN.
MAKES: 4 SERVINGS

2 cups uncooked instant rice
1 package (16 ounces) frozen broccoli-cauliflower blend, thawed
4 orange roughy fillets (6 ounces each)
1 can (14½ ounces) chicken broth
1 can (14½ ounces) fire-roasted diced tomatoes, undrained
1 teaspoon garlic powder
1 teaspoon lemon-pepper seasoning
¼ to ½ teaspoon cayenne pepper
½ cup shredded cheddar cheese

1. Place rice in a greased 13x9-in. baking dish. Layer with the vegetables and fish. Pour the broth and tomatoes over the top; sprinkle with seasonings.

2. Cover and bake at 375° for 25-30 minutes or until fish flakes easily with a fork and rice is tender. Sprinkle with cheese; bake 5 minutes longer or until cheese is melted.

Corn Bread-Topped Salmon

There's no need to serve bread when you've already baked it into the main course. This economical salmon casserole tastes great with tuna or chicken as well.

—**BILLIE WILSON** MASONIC HOME, KY

PREP: 15 MIN. • **BAKE:** 30 MIN.
MAKES: 6-8 SERVINGS

- 2 cans (10¾ ounces each) condensed cream of mushroom soup, undiluted
- ¼ cup milk
- 1 can (14¾ ounces) salmon, drained, bones and skin removed
- 1½ cups frozen peas, thawed
- 1 package (8½ ounces) corn bread/muffin mix
- 1 jar (4 ounces) diced pimientos, drained
- ¼ cup finely chopped green pepper
- 1 teaspoon finely chopped onion
- ½ teaspoon celery seed
- ¼ teaspoon dried thyme

1. Preheat the oven to 400°. In a large saucepan, bring soup and milk to a boil; add salmon and peas. Pour into a greased shallow 2½-qt. baking dish. Prepare the corn bread batter according to package directions; stir in remaining ingredients. Spoon over salmon mixture.

2. Bake, uncovered, 30-35 minutes or until a toothpick inserted in the corn bread comes out clean.

TOP TIP

Not big on salmon? Try this casserole with canned tuna, imitation lobster or cooked chicken or ham. Swap out the cream of mushroom soup for condensed cheese soup, and replace the salmon with cooked ground beef for a completely new flavor combination.

Scallop Mac & Cheese

Scallops are a nice way to dress up this classic feel-good food. They transform mac and cheese into a delicious and sophisticated dish for grown-up tastes.

—LAURIE LUFKIN ESSEX, MA

PREP: 35 MIN. • **BAKE:** 15 MIN.
MAKES: 5 SERVINGS

- 2 cups uncooked medium pasta shells
- ½ cup butter, divided
- 1 cup French bread baguette crumbs
- 1 pound bay scallops
- 1 cup sliced fresh mushrooms
- 1 small onion, chopped
- 3 tablespoons all-purpose flour
- ¾ teaspoon dried thyme
- ¼ teaspoon salt
- ⅛ teaspoon pepper
- 2 cups whole milk
- ½ cup white wine or chicken broth
- 2 tablespoons sherry or chicken broth
- 1 cup (4 ounces) shredded Swiss cheese
- 1 cup (4 ounces) shredded sharp cheddar cheese

1. Cook pasta according to the package directions. Meanwhile, in a small skillet, melt 4 tablespoons butter. Add bread crumbs; cook and stir until they are lightly toasted.

2. In a large skillet over medium heat, melt 2 tablespoons butter. Add scallops; cook and stir for 2 minutes or until firm and opaque. Remove and keep warm. Melt remaining butter in the pan; add mushrooms and onion. Cook and stir until tender. Stir in the flour, thyme, salt and pepper until blended.

3. Gradually add the milk, wine and sherry. Bring to a boil; cook and stir for 1-2 minutes or until thickened. Stir in cheeses until melted. Drain pasta; stir pasta and scallops into sauce.

4. Divide among five 10-oz. ramekins or custard cups. Sprinkle with bread crumbs. Place ramekins on a baking sheet. Bake, uncovered, at 350° for 15-20 minutes or until heated through. Spoon onto plates if desired.

TOP TIP

Scallops are commonly found in two groups: the sea scallop, yielding 10-20 per pound, or smaller bay scallop, yielding 60-90 per pound. Scallops are usually available shucked, are sold fresh or frozen and range in color from pale beige to creamy pink.

Tuna-Chip Casserole

Here's cheesy comfort food at its best. Try it and see!

—JANIS PLOURDE SMOOTH ROCK FALLS, ON

PREP: 20 MIN. • **BAKE:** 20 MIN.
MAKES: 6 SERVINGS

1 package (7 ounces) plain potato chips, divided
1 can (5 ounces) light tuna in water, drained and flaked
1 package (10½ ounces) frozen asparagus tips, thawed and patted dry or 1 can (15 ounces) asparagus spears, drained and sliced

SAUCE
⅔ cup evaporated milk
1 tablespoon lemon juice
¼ teaspoon ground mustard
⅛ teaspoon white pepper

TOPPING
¼ cup shredded cheddar cheese
½ cup sliced almonds

1. Crush chips and place half in greased 2-qt. baking dish. Arrange tuna over chips. Top with asparagus and the remaining chips. Combine sauce ingredients and pour over top. Sprinkle with cheese and almonds.

2. Bake, uncovered, at 325° for 20-25 minutes or until heated through. Let stand for 5 minutes before serving.

POTLUCK

Seafood-Stuffed Shells

These stuffed shells are so good, we have them regularly. Even if you don't care for most fish recipes, you'll like this one.
—**EZRA WEAVER** WOLCOTT, NY

PREP: 35 MIN. • **BAKE:** 30 MIN.
MAKES: 10 SERVINGS

- 30 uncooked jumbo pasta shells
- ½ pound bay scallops
- 2 teaspoons butter
- 2 eggs
- 2 cups (16 ounces) cream-style cottage cheese
- 1 carton (15 ounces) ricotta cheese
- ½ teaspoon ground nutmeg
- ¼ teaspoon pepper
- 1 can (6 ounces) lump crabmeat, drained
- ¾ pound cooked small shrimp, peeled and deveined
- 1 jar (15 ounces) Alfredo sauce

1. Cook the pasta shells according to the package directions.

2. Meanwhile, in a small skillet over medium heat, cook scallops in butter 1-2 minutes or until opaque. Transfer to a large bowl.

3. Preheat oven to 350°. Place one egg and half the cottage cheese, ricotta, nutmeg and pepper in a blender; cover and process until smooth. Add to the scallops. Repeat with the remaining egg, cottage cheese, ricotta, nutmeg and pepper. Add to the scallops. Stir in crab and shrimp.

4. Drain shells and rinse in cold water. Stuff with seafood mixture. Place in a greased 13x9-in. baking dish. Top with Alfredo sauce.

5. Cover and bake 30-35 minutes or until bubbly.

Seafood in Tomato Sauce

We live near the Chesapeake Bay and reap its bountiful seafood harvest. I serve this to company often and receive rave reviews every time. I hope you'll enjoy it as much as my family does.

—**JEFFREY MACCORD** NEW CASTLE, DE

PREP: 20 MIN. • **COOK:** 45 MIN.
MAKES: 4 SERVINGS

- 1¾ cups sliced fresh mushrooms
- 1 garlic clove, minced
- 3 tablespoons canola oil, divided
- 1 can (14½ ounces) diced tomatoes, drained
- 1½ teaspoons dried oregano
- 1 teaspoon sugar
- 1 teaspoon dried thyme
  Salt and pepper to taste
- ½ pound lump crabmeat or imitation crabmeat
- ½ pound bay scallops
- ½ pound uncooked small shrimp, peeled and deveined
- 1 cup cooked long grain rice
- ¾ cup shredded Parmesan cheese

1. In a large saucepan, saute the mushrooms and garlic in 1 tablespoon oil for 3-4 minutes. Add the tomatoes, oregano, sugar, thyme, salt and pepper.

2. Bring to a boil. Reduce heat; cook and simmer for 30 minutes. Uncover; cook 10 minutes longer. Remove from the heat; stir in crab.

3. Meanwhile, in a large skillet, cook the scallops and shrimp in the remaining oil until the shrimp are pink and scallops are opaque.

4. Divide the rice among four individual baking dishes. Top with the shrimp and scallops. Spoon tomato mixture over rice and sprinkle with Parmesan cheese. Bake at 350° for 10 minutes or until heated through and cheese is melted.

HOW TO

PEEL AND DEVEIN SHRIMP

❶ Start on the underside by the head area to remove the shell from shrimp. Pull legs and first section of shell to one side. Continue pulling shell up around the top and to the other side. Pull off shell by tail if desired.

❷ Remove the black vein running down the back of shrimp by making a shallow slit with a paring knife along the back from the head area to the tail.

❸ Rinse shrimp under cold water to remove the vein.

Crab 'n' Penne Casserole

Purchased Alfredo sauce makes this casserole creamy while pepper flakes kick up the taste. As an added bonus, summer squash and zucchini lend garden-fresh goodness.

—BERNADETTE BENNETT WACO, TX

PREP: 20 MIN. • **BAKE:** 40 MIN.
MAKES: 6 SERVINGS

1½ cups uncooked penne pasta
1 jar (15 ounces) Alfredo sauce
1½ cups imitation crabmeat, chopped
1 medium yellow summer squash, sliced
1 medium zucchini, sliced
1 tablespoon dried parsley flakes
⅛ to ¼ teaspoon crushed red pepper flakes
1½ cups (6 ounces) shredded part-skim mozzarella cheese
2 tablespoons dry bread crumbs
2 teaspoons butter, melted

1. Preheat oven to 325°. Cook the pasta according to the package directions.

2. Iin a large bowl, combine Alfredo sauce, crab, yellow squash, zucchini, parsley and pepper flakes. Drain pasta; add to the sauce mixture and toss to coat. Transfer to a greased 13x9-in. baking dish. Sprinkle with cheese.

3. Cover and bake 35 minutes or until heated through. Toss bread crumbs and butter; sprinkle over casserole. Bake, uncovered, 5-6 minutes longer or until browned.

Cheesy Fish Fillets with Spinach

If you have trouble coaxing children to eat spinach, this fast-to-fix dish might be the solution. The homemade cheese sauce works for me every time!

—MARLA BRENNEMAN GOSHEN, IN

PREP: 20 MIN. • **BAKE:** 25 MIN.
MAKES: 4 SERVINGS

- 2 tablespoons butter
- 2 tablespoons all-purpose flour
- 1 teaspoon chicken bouillon granules
  Dash nutmeg
  Dash cayenne pepper
  Dash white pepper
- 1 cup milk
- 2/3 cup shredded cheddar or shredded Swiss cheese
- 1 package (10 ounces) frozen chopped spinach, thawed and well-drained
- 1 tablespoon lemon juice
- 1 pound cod, cut into 3/4-inch pieces
- 1/2 teaspoon salt
- 2 tablespoons grated Parmesan cheese
  Paprika

1. In a large skillet, melt butter. Stir in the flour, bouillon, nutmeg, cayenne and the white pepper until smooth. Gradually stir in milk. Bring to a boil; cook and stir for 1-2 minutes or until thickened. Stir in the cheddar cheese until melted; set aside.

2. Place the spinach in an ungreased 8-in.-square baking dish. Sprinkle with lemon juice. Arrange fish on spinach; sprinkle with salt. Spoon sauce over top.

3. Bake, uncovered, at 350° for 20-25 minutes or until fish flakes easily with a fork. Sprinkle with Parmesan cheese and paprika; bake 5 minutes longer or until lightly browned.

POTLUCK

Oven Jambalaya

If you're looking for an easy but delicious version of jambalaya, this is it!

—RUBY WILLIAMS BOGALUSA, LA

PREP: 10 MIN. • **BAKE:** 1 HOUR
MAKES: 8-10 SERVINGS

$2\frac{1}{4}$ cups water
$1\frac{1}{2}$ cups uncooked long grain rice
  1 can ($10\frac{3}{4}$ ounces) condensed cream of celery soup, undiluted
  1 can ($10\frac{3}{4}$ ounces) condensed cream of onion soup, undiluted
  1 can (10 ounces) diced tomatoes and green chilies, undrained
  1 pound smoked sausage, cut into $\frac{1}{2}$-inch slices
  1 pound cooked medium shrimp, peeled and deveined

1. In a large bowl, combine the first five ingredients. Transfer mixture to a greased 13x9-in. baking dish.

2. Cover and bake at 350° for 40 minutes. Stir in sausage and shrimp. Cover and bake 20-30 minutes longer or until the rice is tender.

TOP TIP

Some like it hot...jambalaya, that is! Spice up your dinner by adding a few drops of hot sauce or a dash of red pepper flakes to this jambalaya before popping it in the oven. If you prefer milder food, use a can of plain diced tomatoes and not those with green chilies.

Seafood Casserole

A family favorite, this rice casserole is stuffed with plenty of seafood and veggies. It's hearty, homey and so easy to make.
—**NANCY BILLUPS** PRINCETON, IA

PREP: 20 MIN. • **BAKE:** 40 MIN.
MAKES: 6 SERVINGS

- 1 package (6 ounces) long grain and wild rice
- 1 pound frozen crabmeat, thawed or 2½ cups canned lump crabmeat, drained
- 1 pound cooked medium shrimp, peeled, deveined and cut into ½-inch pieces
- 2 celery ribs, chopped
- 1 medium onion, finely chopped
- ½ cup finely chopped green pepper
- 1 can (4 ounces) mushroom stems and pieces, drained
- 1 jar (2 ounces) diced pimientos, drained
- 1 cup mayonnaise
- 1 cup 2% milk
- ½ teaspoon pepper
  Dash Worcestershire sauce
- ¼ cup dry bread crumbs

1. Cook rice according to package directions. Meanwhile, preheat oven to 375°.

2. In a large bowl, combine the crab, shrimp, celery, onion, green pepper, mushrooms and pimientos. In a small bowl, whisk the mayonnaise, milk, pepper and Worcestershire sauce; stir into seafood mixture. Stir in rice.

3. Transfer to a greased 13x9-in. baking dish. Sprinkle with bread crumbs. Bake, uncovered, 40-50 minutes or until bubbly.

Sweet Potato
Chili Bake, p. 179

CHAPTER 7

MEATLESS CHOICES

You won't miss the meat in these flavor-packed favorites.

Grilled Cheese & Tomato Soup Bake

This casserole brings together two classic comfort foods—grilled cheese sandwiches and tomato soup. Even my picky-eater husband devours it.

—MORGAN SEGER ANSONIA, OH

PREP: 25 MIN. • **BAKE:** 25 MIN. + STANDING
MAKES: 6 SERVINGS

- 3 ounces reduced-fat cream cheese
- 1½ teaspoons dried basil, divided
- 12 slices Italian, sourdough or rye bread (½ inch thick)
- 6 slices part-skim mozzarella cheese
- 6 tablespoons butter, softened
- ½ cup tomato paste
- 1 garlic clove, minced
- ¼ teaspoon salt
- ¼ teaspoon pepper
- 1¾ cups 2% milk
- 2 eggs
- 1 cup (4 ounces) shredded Italian cheese blend or part-skim mozzarella cheese

1. Preheat oven to 350°. In a small bowl, mix cream cheese and 1 teaspoon basil until blended; spread onto six bread slices. Top with mozzarella cheese and remaining bread.

2. Spread outsides of sandwiches with butter. Arrange in a greased 13x9-in. baking dish.

3. In a small saucepan, combine tomato paste, garlic, salt, pepper and remaining basil; cook and stir over medium heat 1 minute. Gradually whisk in milk; bring to a boil. Reduce heat; simmer, uncovered, 4-5 minutes or until thickened, stirring frequently. Remove from heat.

4. Whisk eggs in a large bowl; gradually whisk in a third of the milk mixture. Stir in remaining milk mixture; pour over sandwiches. Sprinkle with the Italian cheese blend.

5. Bake, uncovered, 25-30 minutes or until golden brown and cheese is melted. Let stand 10 minutes before serving.

Broccoli Mac & Cheese Bake

My husband prepared a variation of this made-from-scratch macaroni and cheese for me on our first date. Over the years, we've tweaked the recipe to suit our tastes. Now we think it's better than ever!
—**LISA DEMARSH** MT. SOLON, VA

PREP: 25 MIN. • **BAKE:** 20 MIN.
MAKES: 12 SERVINGS

- 3 cups uncooked elbow macaroni
- 4 cups fresh broccoli florets
- 1/2 cup butter, cubed
- 3 tablespoons all-purpose flour
- 1/2 teaspoon garlic powder
- 1/2 teaspoon onion powder
- 1/4 teaspoon pepper
- 1/8 teaspoon salt
- 2 cans (12 ounces each) evaporated milk
- 2 1/2 cups (10 ounces) shredded cheddar cheese, divided
- 1/2 cup crushed cornbread-flavored crackers (about 6 crackers)

1. Cook macaroni according to package directions, adding broccoli during the last 3-4 minutes; drain.

2. In a large saucepan, melt the butter. Stir in the flour, garlic powder, onion powder, pepper and salt until smooth; gradually stir in evaporated milk. Bring to a boil; cook and stir for 2 minutes or until thickened. Remove from the heat; stir in 2 cups cheese.

3. Place half of macaroni and broccoli in a greased 13x9-in. baking dish. Top with half of the cheese sauce. Repeat layers. Sprinkle with the cracker crumbs and remaining cheese.

4. Bake, uncovered, at 375° for 20-25 minutes or until bubbly.

FREEZE IT

Make-Ahead Spinach Manicotti

Friends and family often request this saucy spinach manicotti because it's just that good. The shells are stuffed before cooking, which means I can assemble them the night before and focus more on my guests the next day.
—**CHRISTY FREEMAN** CENTRAL POINT, OR

PREP: 20 MIN. + CHILLING • **BAKE:** 40 MIN.
MAKES: 7 SERVINGS

1   carton (15 ounces) whole-milk
        ricotta cheese
1   package (10 ounces) frozen chopped
        spinach, thawed and squeezed dry
1½   cups (6 ounces) shredded part-skim
        mozzarella cheese, divided
¾   cup shredded Parmesan cheese,
        divided
1   egg, lightly beaten
2   teaspoons minced fresh parsley
½   teaspoon onion powder
½   teaspoon pepper
⅛   teaspoon garlic powder
3   jars (24 ounces each) spaghetti
        sauce
1   cup water
1   package (8 ounces) manicotti shells

1. In a large bowl, mix ricotta, spinach, 1 cup mozzarella cheese, ¼ cup Parmesan cheese, egg, parsley and seasonings. In a large bowl, mix the spaghetti sauce and water; spread 1 cup into a greased 13x9-in. baking dish.

2. Fill the uncooked manicotti shells with ricotta mixture; arrange over spaghetti sauce mixture. Pour remaining spaghetti sauce mixture over top. Sprinkle with remaining mozzarella and Parmesan cheeses. Refrigerate, covered, overnight.

3. Remove from refrigerator 30 minutes before baking. Preheat the oven to 350°. Bake, uncovered, 40-50 minutes or until manicotti is tender.

FREEZE OPTION Cover and freeze the unbaked casserole. To use, partially thaw in refrigerator overnight. Remove from refrigerator 30 minutes before baking. Preheat oven to 350°. Bake casserole as directed, increasing time as necessary to heat through and for a thermometer inserted in center to read 165°.

Hearty Tomato-Olive Penne

Who needs meat when you have a pasta dish loaded with tomatoes, olives and Havarti cheese? I often assemble it in advance and pop it into the oven the next day, adding a few minutes to the baking time.

—**JACQUELINE FRANK** GREEN BAY, WI

PREP: 50 MIN. • **BAKE:** 25 MIN.
MAKES: 8 SERVINGS

- 2 large onions, chopped
- 6 tablespoons olive oil
- 3 garlic cloves, minced
- 3 pounds plum tomatoes, seeded and chopped (about 10 tomatoes)
- 1 cup vegetable or chicken broth
- 1 tablespoon dried basil
- 1 teaspoon crushed red pepper flakes
- 1/2 teaspoon salt
- 1/4 teaspoon pepper
- 1 package (16 ounces) uncooked penne pasta
- 1 block (24 ounces) Havarti cheese, cut into 1/2-in. cubes
- 1 cup pitted Greek olives
- 1/3 cup grated Parmesan cheese

1. In a Dutch oven, saute onions in oil until tender. Add garlic; cook 1 minute longer. Stir in tomatoes, broth, basil, pepper flakes, salt and pepper. Bring to a boil. Reduce heat; cover and simmer 25-30 minutes or until sauce is slightly thickened.

2. Meanwhile, cook the penne pasta according to package directions; drain.

3. Preheat oven to 375°. Stir the Havarti cheese, Greek olives and cooked penne pasta into sauce. Transfer to a greased 13x9-in. baking dish; sprinkle with the Parmesan cheese.

4. Cover and bake 20 minutes. Uncover; bake 5 minutes longer or until cheese is melted.

TOP TIP

Seeding a tomato not only removes the seeds, but also eliminates some of the juice that can make a casserole watery. To seed a tomato, cut it in half and gently squeeze each half. If you don't want to lose as much juice, try using a small spoon to scoop out the seeds.

Cheesy Chili Casserole

A short list of ingredients packs plenty of flavor into this easy casserole. Serve it as the star of your next meal.

—**PHYLLIS BIDWELL** LAS VEGAS, NV

PREP: 10 MIN. • **BAKE:** 40 MIN.
MAKES: 8 SERVINGS

- 2 cups (8 ounces) shredded Monterey Jack cheese
- 2 cups (8 ounces) shredded cheddar cheese
- 1 can (7 ounces) whole green chilies, rinsed and seeded
- 2 eggs
- 2 tablespoons all-purpose flour
- 1 can (12 ounces) evaporated milk
- 1 can (8 ounces) tomato sauce or 1 cup fresh salsa, drained, divided

1. In a large bowl, combine cheeses. In a greased 11x7-in. baking dish, layer cheese and chilies. Whisk the eggs, flour and milk; pour over cheese mixture.

2. Bake at 350° for 30 minutes. Top with half the tomato sauce or salsa; bake 10 minutes longer or until heated through. Let stand for 5 minutes before serving. Serve with remaining sauce.

Zucchini Enchiladas

When my garden is bursting with zucchini, I turn to this recipe to make the most of it.
—**ANGELA LEINENBACH** MECHANICSVLLE, VA

PREP: 1½ HOURS • **BAKE:** 30 MIN.
MAKES: 12 SERVINGS

- 1 medium sweet yellow pepper, chopped
- 1 medium green pepper, chopped
- 1 large sweet onion, chopped
- 2 tablespoons olive oil
- 2 garlic cloves, minced
- 2 cans (15 ounces each) tomato sauce
- 2 cans (14½ ounces each) no-salt-added diced tomatoes, undrained
- 2 tablespoons chili powder
- 2 teaspoons sugar
- 2 teaspoons dried marjoram
- 1 teaspoon dried basil
- 1 teaspoon ground cumin
- ¼ teaspoon salt
- ¼ teaspoon cayenne pepper
- 1 bay leaf
- 3 pounds zucchini, shredded (about 8 cups)
- 24 corn tortillas (6 inches), warmed
- 4 cups (16 ounces) shredded reduced-fat cheddar cheese
- 2 cans (2¼ ounces each) sliced ripe olives, drained
- ½ cup minced fresh cilantro
  Reduced-fat sour cream, optional

1. In a large saucepan, saute peppers and onion in oil until tender. Add garlic; cook 1 minute longer. Stir in the tomato sauce, tomatoes, chili powder, sugar, marjoram, basil, cumin, salt, cayenne and bay leaf. Bring to a boil. Reduce heat; simmer, uncovered, 30-35 minutes or until slightly thickened. Discard bay leaf.

2. Preheat oven to 350°. Place ⅓ cup zucchini down the center of each corn tortilla; top with 2 tablespoons cheese and 2 teaspoons olives. Roll up and place seam side down in two 13x9-in. baking dishes coated with cooking spray. Pour the sauce over the top; sprinkle with the remaining cheese.

3. Bake, uncovered, 30-35 minutes or until heated through. Sprinkle with cilantro. Serve with sour cream if desired.

Ravioli Casserole

It takes less than 30 minutes to prep this hearty, crowd-pleasing dinner. Nutmeg, white wine and basil give it an extra-special flavor you can't help but love.

—MARGIE WILLIAMS MT. JULIET, TN

PREP: 25 MIN. • **BAKE:** 35 MIN. + STANDING
MAKES: 8 SERVINGS

---

1 package (25 ounces) frozen cheese ravioli
¼ cup butter, cubed
¼ cup all-purpose flour
¼ teaspoon salt
¼ teaspoon ground nutmeg
2 cups milk
¼ cup white wine or vegetable broth
½ cup minced fresh basil
3 cups (12 ounces) shredded part-skim mozzarella cheese, divided
¾ cup grated Parmesan cheese, divided
2½ cups marinara or spaghetti sauce

1. Cook the ravioli according to package directions.

2. Meanwhile, in a large saucepan, melt butter. Stir in the flour, salt and nutmeg until smooth; gradually add the milk and wine. Bring to a boil; cook and stir for 1 minute or until thickened. Remove from heat. Stir in basil, 1 cup mozzarella cheese and ¼ cup Parmesan cheese.

3. Drain ravioli; toss with sauce mixture. Transfer to a greased 13x9-in. baking dish. Top with 1 cup mozzarella cheese and marinara sauce; sprinkle with the remaining cheeses.

4. Cover and bake at 375° for 30 minutes. Uncover; bake 5-10 minutes longer or until bubbly. Let stand for 15 minutes before serving.

Vegetarian Potato au Gratin

Fill up on veggies and load up on great taste with this creamy, hearty casserole. You'll appreciate the homey bread-crumb topping and hands-free bake time at the end of a long day.
—*TASTE OF HOME* TEST KITCHEN

PREP: 15 MIN. • **BAKE:** 50 MIN. + STANDING
MAKES: 6 SERVINGS

  3 medium carrots, thinly sliced
  1 medium green pepper, chopped
  4 tablespoons butter, divided
  3 tablespoons all-purpose flour
  1 teaspoon dried oregano
 ½ teaspoon salt
2½ cups 2% milk
  1 can (15 ounces) black beans, rinsed and drained
  3 cups (12 ounces) shredded Swiss cheese, divided
  4 medium Yukon Gold potatoes, thinly sliced
 ½ cup seasoned bread crumbs

1. Preheat oven to 400°. In a large saucepan, saute carrots and pepper in 3 tablespoons butter until tender. Stir in flour, oregano and salt until blended; gradually add milk. Bring to a boil; cook and stir 2 minutes or until thickened. Stir in beans and 2 cups cheese until cheese is melted.

2. Layer half of the potatoes and sauce in a greased 13x9-in. baking dish; repeat the layers. Sprinkle with the remaining cheese. In a microwave, melt the remaining butter. Stir in bread crumbs. Sprinkle over top.

3. Cover and bake 50-55 minutes. Let stand 10 minutes before serving.

Sweet Potato Chili Bake

Sweet potatoes and black beans add robust flavor and earthiness to this vegetarian chili.
—**JILLIAN TOURNOUX** MASSILLON, OH

PREP: 30 MIN. • **BAKE:** 20 MIN.
MAKES: 7 SERVINGS

- 2 cups cubed peeled sweet potato
- 1 medium sweet red pepper, chopped
- 1 tablespoon olive oil
- 1 garlic clove, minced
- 1 can (28 ounces) diced tomatoes, undrained
- 2 cups vegetable broth
- 1 can (15 ounces) black beans, rinsed and drained
- 4½ teaspoons brown sugar
- 3 teaspoons chili powder
- 1 teaspoon salt
- ½ teaspoon pepper
- 1 package (6½ ounces) corn bread/ muffin mix
- ½ cup shredded cheddar cheese
  Optional toppings: sour cream, shredded cheddar cheese and chopped seeded jalapeno pepper

1. In an ovenproof Dutch oven, saute sweet potato and red pepper in oil until crisp-tender. Add garlic; cook 1 minute longer. Add tomatoes, vegetable broth, beans, brown sugar, chili powder, salt and pepper. Bring to a boil. Reduce the heat; simmer, uncovered, 15-20 minutes or until potatoes are tender.

2. Meanwhile, preheat the oven to 400°. Prepare the corn bread batter according to the package directions; stir in cheese. Drop by tablespoonfuls over chili.

3. Cover and bake 18-20 minutes or until a toothpick inserted in center comes out clean. Serve with toppings of your choice.

NOTE Wear disposable gloves when cutting hot peppers; the oils can burn skin. Avoid touching your face.

Eggplant Parmesan

Because this recipe calls for baking the eggplant instead of frying it, it's healthier than the traditional dish. The prep time is a little longer than for some recipes, but the wonderful Italian flavors and rustic elegance make it worth the extra effort.

—**LACI HOOTEN** MCKINNEY, TX

PREP: 40 MIN. • **COOK:** 25 MIN.
MAKES: 8 SERVINGS

- 3 eggs, beaten
- 2½ cups panko (Japanese) bread crumbs
- 3 medium eggplants, cut into ¼-inch slices
- 2 jars (4½ ounces each) sliced mushrooms, drained
- ½ teaspoon dried basil
- ⅛ teaspoon dried oregano
- 2 cups (8 ounces) shredded part-skim mozzarella cheese
- ½ cup grated Parmesan cheese
- 1 jar (28 ounces) spaghetti sauce

1. Preheat oven to 350°. Place eggs and panko bread crumbs in separate shallow bowls. Dip eggplant in eggs, then coat in panko bread crumbs. Place on baking sheets coated with cooking spray. Bake 15-20 minutes or until tender and golden brown, turning once.

2. In a small bowl, combine mushrooms, basil and oregano. In another small bowl, combine mozzarella cheese and Parmesan cheese.

3. Spread ½ cup sauce into a 13x9-in. baking dish coated with cooking spray. Layer with a third of the mushroom mixture, a third of the eggplant, ¾ cup sauce and a third of the cheese mixture. Repeat layers twice.

4. Bake, uncovered, at 350° for 25-30 minutes or until heated through and cheese is melted.

TOP TIP

Purchase eggplants with smooth skin; avoid those with soft or brown spots. Refrigerate eggplants for up to 5 days in a plastic bag. Young and tender eggplants do not need to be peeled before using, but larger eggplants may be bitter and will taste better when peeled.

**Chicken Cheese
Strata, p. 192**

CHAPTER 8

READY IN 30

From start to finish, these recipes take just half an hour to fix.

Frito Pie

Frito pie is legendary in Southwestern states for being spicy, crunchy, cheesy—just plain fabulous! Here's my easy version that takes advantage of convenient canned enchilada sauce and seasoned pinto beans. During baking, toss together a simple green salad to serve on the side. A scoop of sherbet is a refreshing way to top off the meal.

—**JAN MOON** ALAMOGORDO, NM

START TO FINISH: 30 MIN.
MAKES: 6 SERVINGS

- 1 pound ground beef
- 1 medium onion, chopped
- 2 cans (15 ounces each) Ranch Style beans (pinto beans in seasoned tomato sauce)
- 1 package (9¾ ounces) Fritos corn chips
- 2 cans (10 ounces each) enchilada sauce
- 2 cups (8 ounces) shredded cheddar cheese
  Thinly sliced green onions, optional

1. Preheat oven to 350°. In a large skillet, cook beef and onion over medium heat 6-8 minutes or until beef is no longer pink and onion is tender, breaking up beef into crumbles; drain. Stir in beans; heat through.

2. Reserve 1 cup corn chips for topping. Place remaining corn chips in a greased 13x9-in. baking dish. Layer with the meat mixture, enchilada sauce and cheddar cheese; top with reserved chips.

3. Bake, uncovered, 15-20 minutes or until the cheese is melted. If desired, sprinkle with green onions.

TOP TIP

Store unwashed green onions in a plastic bag in the crisper drawer of your refrigerator for 1-2 weeks. When you're making a recipe that calls for sliced green onions and you don't want to dirty a cutting board, just snip the amount you need using kitchen scissors.

Wild Rice Chicken Dinner

With tender chunks of chicken, green beans and rice, this casserole has everything you need for a hungry family. Water chestnuts and almonds add a nice crunch, too.

—**LORRAINE HANSON** INDEPENDENCE, IA

START TO FINISH: 30 MIN.
MAKES: 2 CASSEROLES
(6-8 SERVINGS EACH)

- 2 packages (8.8 ounces each) ready-to-serve long grain and wild rice
- 2 packages (16 ounces each) frozen French-style green beans, thawed
- 2 cans (10¾ ounces each) condensed cream of celery soup, undiluted
- 2 cans (8 ounces each) sliced water chestnuts, drained
- ⅔ cup chopped onion
- 2 jars (4 ounces each) sliced pimientos, drained
- 1 cup mayonnaise
- ½ cup 2% milk
- 1 teaspoon pepper
- 6 cups cubed cooked chicken
- 1 cup slivered almonds, divided

1. Heat the rice according to the package directions. Meanwhile, in a Dutch oven, combine the green beans, cream of celery soup, water chestnuts, onion, pimientos, mayonnaise, milk and pepper. Bring to a boil. Reduce heat; cover and simmer for 5 minutes. Stir in chicken and rice; cook 3-4 minutes longer or until the chicken is heated through.

2. Transfer half of mixture to a serving dish; sprinkle with ½ cup almonds. Serve immediately. Pour remaining mixture into a greased 13x9-in. baking dish; cool. Sprinkle with remaining almonds. Cover and freeze for up to 3 months.

TO USE FROZEN CASSEROLE Thaw the casserole in the refrigerator overnight. Cover and bake at 350° for 40-45 minutes or until heated through.

HOW TO

MAKE CUBED COOKED CHICKEN

❶ To prepare cubed cooked chicken for use in recipes, simmer boneless chicken breasts in a little water seasoned with salt, pepper and your favorite herbs as desired.

❷ Cool and dice the chicken; store it in the freezer to use in recipes as needed.

Mama Mia Meatball Taquitos

We love lasagna, but it can take too long to make on busy weeknights. My solution is Italian-style meatball taquitos. My children get the flavors they crave, and I get a delicious dinner on the table in a hurry. It's win-win!

—**LAUREN WYLER** DRIPPING SPRINGS, TX

START TO FINISH: 30 MIN.
MAKES: 6 SERVINGS

- 12 frozen fully cooked Italian turkey meatballs, thawed
- 2 cups (8 ounces) shredded part-skim mozzarella cheese
- 1 cup whole-milk ricotta cheese
- 1 teaspoon Italian seasoning
- 12 flour tortillas (8 inches)
  Cooking spray
  Warm marinara sauce

1. Preheat oven to 425°. Place turkey meatballs in a food processor; pulse until finely chopped. Transfer to a large bowl; stir in cheeses and Italian seasoning.

2. Spread about ¼ cup meatball mixture down the center of each flour tortilla. Roll up tightly. Place on a greased 15x10x1-in. baking pan, seam side down; spritz with cooking spray.

3. Bake 16-20 minutes or until golden brown. Serve with marinara sauce.

Pepperoni Pizza Casserole

Egg noodles make a great crust for a pizza casserole and don't need to rise like dough does. If you prefer your pies loaded, pile this dish with sausage, peppers, onions or other popular toppings. I've even arranged different ingredients on opposite sides of the pan so we can all have our favorites!
—**CATHERINE YEATS** LEWISTON, ID

START TO FINISH: 30 MIN.
MAKES: 8 SERVINGS

1   package (16 ounces) wide egg
     noodles
2¼ cups pizza sauce, divided
1   cup sliced fresh mushrooms
1   can (2¼ ounces) sliced ripe olives,
     drained
1   package (3½ ounces) sliced
     pepperoni
2   cups (8 ounces) shredded part-skim
     mozzarella cheese

1. Cook the egg noodles according to the package directions; drain. In a large bowl, combine egg noodles and ¾ cup pizza sauce. Transfer to a greased 13x9-in. baking dish. Top with the remaining pizza sauce.

2. Layer with the mushrooms, ripe olives and pepperoni. Sprinkle with shredded mozzarella cheese. Bake, uncovered, at 375° for 15-18 minutes or until heated through and the cheese is melted.

HOW TO

PREPARE FRESH MUSHROOMS
Gently remove dirt from fresh mushrooms by rubbing them with a mushroom brush or damp paper towel. Or quickly rinse the mushrooms under cold water, drain them and pat them dry with paper towels. (Do not peel mushrooms.) Trim the stems.

Chicken Cheese Strata

This simple strata of chicken, broccoli, cubed bread and cheese may seem ordinary at first. But it gets a family-pleasing flavor boost from spices and cream of onion soup.
—*TASTE OF HOME* **TEST KITCHEN**

START TO FINISH: 30 MIN.
MAKES: 8 SERVINGS

¾   pound boneless skinless chicken breasts, cut into ½-inch cubes
4   tablespoons butter, divided
3   cups frozen broccoli florets, thawed
½   teaspoon onion salt
½   teaspoon dried thyme
½   teaspoon dried rosemary, crushed
¼   teaspoon pepper
6   cups cubed French bread
2   eggs
¾   cup 2% milk
⅔   cup condensed cream of onion soup, undiluted
1   cup (4 ounces) shredded Colby-Monterey Jack cheese

1. Preheat oven to 400°. In a 10-in. ovenproof skillet, saute the chicken in 2 tablespoons butter until no longer pink. Add broccoli, onion salt, thyme, rosemary and pepper; heat through. Remove from skillet and keep warm.

2. In the same skillet, toast the bread cubes in remaining butter until lightly browned. In a small bowl, combine the eggs, milk and cream of onion soup; pour over the bread cubes. Stir in the chicken mixture. Sprinkle with cheese.

3. Bake, uncovered, 15-20 minutes or until a knife inserted near the center comes out clean. Let stand 5 minutes before cutting.

TOP TIP

Have extra bread? Use it to make croutons. Cube the bread and place it on a baking pan. Drizzle on melted butter and season the cubes with garlic powder and seasoned salt; toss to coat. Bake at 350° until the croutons are lightly browned. Turn off the oven and let them dry.

Biscuit Turkey Bake

When I was a college student, I looked for comforting foods that were easy on the budget. Here's a dinner that met both requirements. I've made it many times for friends' birthdays.
—**STEPHANIE DENNING** MOUNT PLEASANT, IA

START TO FINISH: 30 MIN.
MAKES: 5 SERVINGS

- 1 can (10¾ ounces) condensed cream of chicken soup, undiluted
- 1 cup chopped cooked turkey or chicken
- 1 can (4 ounces) mushroom stems and pieces, drained
- ½ cup frozen peas
- ¼ cup 2% milk
  Dash each ground cumin, dried basil and thyme
- 1 tube (12 ounces) refrigerated buttermilk biscuits

1. Preheat oven to 350°. In a large bowl, combine cream soup, turkey, mushrooms, peas, milk and seasonings. Pour into a greased 8-in.-square baking dish; arrange biscuits over the top.

2. Bake, uncovered, 20-25 minutes or until the biscuits are golden brown.

Spicy Shepherd's Pie

Taco seasoning, chili powder and Mexicorn bring Southwest zip to classic shepherd's pie. It's easy to top with instant mashed potatoes, which I stir up while browning the beef.
—**MARY MALCHOW** NEENAH, WI

START TO FINISH: 30 MIN.
MAKES: 4-6 SERVINGS

1	package (6.6 ounces) instant mashed potatoes
1	pound ground beef
1	medium onion, chopped
1	can (14½ ounces) diced tomatoes, undrained
1	can (11 ounces) Mexicorn, drained
1	can (2¼ ounces) sliced ripe olives, drained
1	envelope taco seasoning
1½	teaspoons chili powder
½	teaspoon salt
⅛	teaspoon garlic powder
1	cup (4 ounces) shredded cheddar cheese, divided

1. Prepare mashed potatoes according to the package directions. Meanwhile, in a large skillet, cook the beef and onion over medium heat until meat is no longer pink, breaking meat into crumbles; drain. Add the tomatoes, corn, ripe olives, taco seasoning, chili powder, salt and garlic powder. Bring to a boil; cook and stir for 1-2 minutes.

2. Transfer to a greased 2½-qt. baking dish. Top with ¾ cup cheese. Spread mashed potatoes over the top; sprinkle with remaining cheese. Bake, uncovered, at 350° for 12-15 minutes or until cheese is melted.

NOTE You may substitute 4½ cups hot homemade mashed potatoes for the instant potatoes if desired.

Beef & Biscuit Bake

Spiced-up ground beef and beans become comfort food at its best when you add a top layer of buttery, cornmeal-coated biscuits. Even hearty appetites are sure to be satisfied.
—**ERIN SCHNEIDER** ST. PETERS, MO

START TO FINISH: 30 MIN.
MAKES: 6-8 SERVINGS

1 pound ground beef
1 can (16 ounces) kidney beans, rinsed and drained
1 can (15¼ ounces) whole kernel corn, drained
1 can (10¾ ounces) condensed tomato soup, undiluted
¼ cup milk
2 tablespoons finely chopped onion
½ teaspoon chili powder
¼ teaspoon salt
1 cup cubed process cheese (Velveeta)
1 tube (12 ounces) refrigerated biscuits
2 to 3 tablespoons butter, melted
⅓ cup yellow cornmeal

1. Preheat oven to 375°. In a saucepan over medium heat, cook the beef until no longer pink, breaking the beef into crumbles; drain. Add the kidney beans, corn, soup, milk, onion, chili powder and salt; bring to a boil. Remove from heat; stir in the cheese until melted. Spoon into a greased 2½-qt. baking dish. Bake, uncovered, 10 minutes.

2. Meanwhile, brush all sides of biscuits with butter; roll in cornmeal. Place on top of bubbling meat mixture. Return to oven 10-12 minutes or until biscuits are lightly browned and cooked through.

DID YOU KNOW?

Cornmeal can be white, yellow or blue depending on which strain of corn is used. Traditionally, white cornmeal is the preferred variety in the South and yellow is more popular in the North. Blue cornmeal can be found in specialty stores. All three types may be used interchangeably in recipes.

Pasta and Sausage Bake

I'm always happy when I get requests for this sausage-filled mostaccioli casserole because it's popular with everyone and smells wonderful while baking. The fact that the recipe requires just five simple ingredients doesn't hurt, either!

—JANET ROEHRING MARBLE FALLS, TX

START TO FINISH: 30 MIN.
MAKES: 4-6 SERVINGS

- 1 pound Italian sausage links
- 1 jar (14 ounces) spaghetti sauce
- 8 ounces mostaccioli, cooked and drained
- 1/3 cup grated Parmesan cheese
- 1 cup (4 ounces) shredded part-skim mozzarella cheese

1. In a large skillet, cook the sausage links over medium heat until a thermometer reads 160°; drain. Slice into 1/2-in. pieces. In a greased 2-qt. baking dish, combine sausage, spaghetti sauce, mostaccioli and Parmesan cheese. Top with mozzarella cheese.

2. Bake, uncovered, at 350° for 15-20 minutes or until heated through.

Salmon Veggie Packets

I think of the cooking of Julia Child when I fix this lemon-pepper salmon *en papillote* (in parchment). It's my first French recipe and makes a wholesome fish dinner.
—**RENEE GREENE** NEW YORK, NY

START TO FINISH: 30 MIN.
MAKES: 4 SERVINGS

- 2 tablespoons white wine
- 1 tablespoon olive oil
- 1/4 teaspoon salt
- 1/4 teaspoon pepper
- 2 medium sweet yellow peppers, julienned
- 2 cups fresh sugar snap peas, trimmed

SALMON

- 2 tablespoons white wine
- 1 tablespoon olive oil
- 1 tablespoon grated lemon peel
- 1/2 teaspoon salt
- 1/4 teaspoon pepper
- 4 salmon fillets (6 ounces each)
- 1 medium lemon, halved

1. Preheat the oven to 400°. Cut four 18x15-in. pieces of parchment paper or heavy-duty foil: fold each crosswise in half, forming a crease. In a large bowl, mix the white wine, oil, salt and pepper. Add vegetables and toss to coat.

2. In a small bowl, mix the first five salmon ingredients. To assemble, lay open one piece of parchment paper; place a salmon fillet on one side. Drizzle with 2 teaspoons white wine mixture; top with one-fourth of the vegetables.

3. Fold paper over fish and vegetables; fold the open ends two times to seal. Repeat with remaining packets. Place on baking sheets.

4. Bake 12-16 minutes or until fish just begins to flake easily with a fork, opening packets carefully to allow steam to escape.

5. To serve, squeeze lemon juice over the vegetables.

**Overnight Brunch
Casserole, p. 208**

CHAPTER 9

LIGHTER FARE

These slimmed-down dishes include complete nutrition facts.

Creamy Tuna-Noodle Casserole

When you want a lighter dinner, try this yummy casserole. I've found it's also good with cooked chicken breast instead of tuna.

—EDIE DESPAIN LOGAN, UT

PREP: 20 MIN. • **BAKE:** 25 MIN.
MAKES: 6 SERVINGS

- 5 cups uncooked egg noodles
- 1 cup frozen peas
- 1 can (10¾ ounces) reduced-fat reduced-sodium condensed cream of mushroom soup, undiluted
- 1 cup (8 ounces) fat-free sour cream
- ⅔ cup grated Parmesan cheese
- ⅓ cup 2% milk
- ¼ teaspoon salt
- 2 cans (5 ounces each) light tuna in water, drained and flaked
- ¼ cup finely chopped onion
- ¼ cup finely chopped green pepper

TOPPING

- ½ cup soft bread crumbs
- 1 tablespoon butter, melted

1. Preheat oven to 350°. Cook the egg noodles according to package directions for al dente, adding peas during the last minute of cooking; drain.

2. Meanwhile, in a large bowl, combine soup, sour cream, cheese, milk and salt; stir in the tuna, onion and green pepper. Add noodles and peas; toss to combine.

3. Transfer to an 11x7-in. baking dish coated with cooking spray. In a small bowl, toss bread crumbs with butter; sprinkle over the top. Bake, uncovered, 25-30 minutes or until bubbly.

NOTE To make soft bread crumbs, tear the bread into pieces and place in a food processor or blender. Cover and pulse until crumbs form. One slice of bread yields ½ to ¾ cup crumbs.

PER SERVING 340 cal., 8 g fat (4 g sat. fat), 63 mg chol., 699 mg sodium, 41 g carb., 3 g fiber, 25 g pro. **Diabetic Exchanges:** 3 starch, 2 lean meat, ½ fat.

POTLUCK

Overnight Brunch Casserole

I love to cook for company and often host brunches. Here's a recipe I've relied on many times. With eggs, ham and a creamy sauce, it stands out from other breakfast casseroles. My guests also appreciate the fact that I use reduced-fat ingredients.

—CANDY HESCH MOSINEE, WI

PREP: 30 MIN. + CHILLING
BAKE: 40 MIN. + STANDING
MAKES: 12 SERVINGS

3	tablespoons butter, divided
2	tablespoons all-purpose flour
1/2	teaspoon salt
1/8	teaspoon pepper
2	cups fat-free milk
5	slices reduced-fat process American cheese product, chopped
1 1/2	cups sliced fresh mushrooms
2	green onions, finely chopped
1	cup cubed fully cooked ham
2	cups egg substitute
4	eggs

TOPPING

3	slices whole wheat bread, cubed
4	teaspoons butter, melted
1/8	teaspoon paprika

1. In a large saucepan, melt 2 tablespoons butter. Stir in flour, salt and pepper until smooth; gradually add milk. Bring to a boil; cook and stir 2 minutes or until slightly thickened. Stir in cheese until melted. Remove from heat.

2. In a large nonstick skillet, saute the mushrooms and onions in remaining butter until tender. Add the ham; heat through. Whisk egg substitute and eggs; add to skillet. Cook and stir until almost set. Stir in cheese sauce.

3. Transfer to a 13x9-in. baking dish coated with cooking spray. Toss bread cubes with butter. Arrange over egg mixture; sprinkle with paprika. Cover and refrigerate overnight.

4. Remove from refrigerator 30 minutes before baking. Preheat oven to 350°. Bake, uncovered, 40-45 minutes or until a knife inserted near the center comes out clean. Let stand 10 minutes before cutting.

PER SERVING 150 cal., 7 g fat (4 g sat. fat), 91 mg chol., 509 mg sodium, 8 g carb., 1 g fiber, 13 g pro. **Diabetic Exchanges:** 2 lean meat, 1 fat, 1/2 starch.

Linguine with Ham & Swiss Cheese

This lightened-up version of linguine casserole cuts nearly half the saturated fat from the original version—without sacrificing the creamy texture or distinctive Swiss cheese flavor.

—MIKE TCHOU PEPPER PIKE, OH

PREP: 15 MIN. • **BAKE:** 45 MIN.
MAKES: 8 SERVINGS

- 8 ounces uncooked whole wheat linguine, broken in half
- 2 cups cubed fully cooked lean ham
- 1¾ cups (7 ounces) shredded Swiss cheese, divided
- 1 can (10¾ ounces) reduced-fat reduced-sodium condensed cream of mushroom soup, undiluted
- 1 cup (8 ounces) reduced-fat sour cream
- 1 medium onion, chopped
- 1 small green pepper, finely chopped

1. Cook the linguine according to the package directions. Meanwhile, in a large bowl, combine the ham, 1½ cups cheese, soup, sour cream, onion and green pepper. Drain pasta; add to ham mixture and stir to coat.

2. Transfer to a 13x9-in. baking dish coated with cooking spray. Cover and bake at 350° for 35 minutes. Uncover; sprinkle with the remaining cheese. Bake 10-15 minutes longer or until cheese is melted.

PER SERVING 293 cal., 12 g fat (7 g sat. fat), 47 mg chol., 665 mg sodium, 29 g carb., 4 g fiber, 19 g pro. **Diabetic Exchanges:** 2 starch, 2 lean meat, 1 fat.

Stacked Vegetables and Ravioli

What a delicious way to use the harvest from your garden! Fresh yellow summer squash, zucchini and basil meet ricotta cheese and ravioli for a saucy Italian specialty. It's great when you want to eat meatless.

—TASTE OF HOME TEST KITCHEN

PREP: 20 MIN. • **BAKE:** 30 MIN. + STANDING
MAKES: 6 SERVINGS

- 2 yellow summer squash
- 2 medium zucchini
- 1 package (9 ounces) refrigerated cheese ravioli
- 1 cup ricotta cheese
- 1 egg
- ½ teaspoon garlic salt
- 1 jar (24 ounces) marinara or spaghetti sauce
- 10 fresh basil leaves, divided
- ¾ cup shredded Parmesan cheese

1. Preheat oven to 350°. Using a vegetable peeler, cut the squash and zucchini into very thin lengthwise strips. In a Dutch oven, cook ravioli according to package directions, adding the vegetable strips during the last 3 minutes of cooking.

2. Meanwhile, in a small bowl, combine the ricotta cheese, egg and garlic salt; set aside. Drain ravioli and vegetables.

3. Spread ½ cup marinara sauce into a greased 11x7-in. baking dish. Layer with half the ravioli and vegetables, half the ricotta mixture, seven basil leaves and 1 cup marinara sauce. Layer with the remaining ravioli, vegetables and sauce. Dollop remaining ricotta mixture over the top; sprinkle with Parmesan cheese.

4. Cover and bake 25 minutes. Uncover and bake 5-10 minutes longer or until cheese is melted. Let stand 10 minutes before cutting. Thinly slice remaining basil; sprinkle over top.

PER SERVING 323 cal., 11 g fat (6 g sat. fat), 76 mg chol., 779 mg sodium, 39 g carb., 4 g fiber, 19 g pro. **Diabetic Exchanges:** 2 starch, 2 medium-fat meat, 1 vegetable.

Beef Tenderloin with Roasted Vegetables

I prepare this for celebrations year-round. The recipe is so convenient because it makes both the tenderloin and a side dish of roasted potatoes, Brussels sprouts and carrots.
—**JANET SINGLETON** BELLEVUE, OH

PREP: 20 MIN. + MARINATING
BAKE: 1 HOUR + STANDING
MAKES: 8-10 SERVINGS

- 1   beef tenderloin roast (3 pounds)
- ¾   cup dry white wine or beef broth
- ¾   cup reduced-sodium soy sauce
- 4   teaspoons minced fresh rosemary
- 4   teaspoons Dijon mustard
- 1½ teaspoons ground mustard
- 3   garlic cloves, peeled and sliced
- 1   pound Yukon Gold potatoes, cut into 1-inch wedges
- 1   pound Brussels sprouts, halved
- 1   pound fresh baby carrots

1. Place the beef tenderloin in a large resealable plastic bag. Combine the white wine, soy sauce, rosemary, Dijon mustard, ground mustard and garlic. Pour half of the marinade over the tenderloin; seal the bag and turn to coat. Refrigerate for 4-12 hours, turning several times. Cover and refrigerate remaining marinade.

2. Place the potatoes, Brussels sprouts and baby carrots in a greased 13x9-in. baking dish; add the reserved marinade and toss to coat. Cover and bake at 425° for 30 minutes; stir.

3. Drain and discard the marinade from the beef tenderloin. Place tenderloin over the vegetables. Bake, uncovered, for 30-45 minutes or until meat reaches the desired doneness (for medium-rare, a thermometer should read 145°; medium, 160°; well-done, 170°).

4. Remove the tenderloin and let stand for 15 minutes. Check the vegetables for doneness. If additional roasting is needed, cover with foil and bake for 10-15 minutes or until tender. Slice the beef and serve with vegetables.

PER SERVING 283 cal., 8 g fat (3 g sat. fat), 60 mg chol., 627 mg sodium, 16 g carb., 3 g fiber, 33 g pro. **Diabetic Exchanges:** 4 lean meat, 1 vegetable, ½ starch.

Chicken-Stuffed Cubanelle Peppers

Here's a new take on traditional stuffed peppers. I substituted shredded cooked chicken for the beef and replaced the usual green peppers with the Cubanelle variety.

—**BEV BURLINGAME** CANTON, OH

PREP: 20 MIN. • **BAKE:** 55 MIN.
MAKES: 6 SERVINGS

- 6 Cubanelle peppers or mild banana peppers
- 2 eggs
- 1 cup salsa
- 3 cups shredded cooked chicken breast
- ¾ cup soft bread crumbs
- ½ cup cooked long grain rice
- 2 cups meatless spaghetti sauce, divided

1. Cut tops off peppers and remove seeds. In a large bowl, combine the eggs, salsa, chicken, bread crumbs and rice. Spoon into peppers.

2. Coat a 13x9-in. baking dish and an 8-in.-square baking dish with cooking spray. Spread 1 cup spaghetti sauce in the larger pan and ½ cup sauce in the smaller pan. Place the peppers over the sauce. Spoon remaining spaghetti sauce over peppers.

3. Cover and bake at 350° for 55-60 minutes or until the peppers are tender.

PER SERVING 230 cal., 4 g fat (1 g sat. fat), 125 mg chol., 661 mg sodium, 20 g carb., 5 g fiber, 26 g pro. **Diabetic Exchanges:** 3 lean meat, 2 vegetable, 1 starch.

Enchilada Casser-Ole!

My whole family likes Mexican food of any kind, but my husband especially loves this casserole. Layered with lean ground beef, beans, tortillas and cheese, it combines all our favorite ingredients in one dish.
—**MARSHA WILLS** HOMOSASSA, FL

PREP: 25 MIN. • **BAKE:** 30 MIN.
MAKES: 8 SERVINGS

- 1 pound lean ground beef (90% lean)
- 1 large onion, chopped
- 2 cups salsa
- 1 can (15 ounces) black beans, rinsed and drained
- ¼ cup reduced-fat Italian salad dressing
- 2 tablespoons reduced-sodium taco seasoning
- ¼ teaspoon ground cumin
- 6 flour tortillas (8 inches)
- ¾ cup reduced-fat sour cream
- 1 cup (4 ounces) shredded reduced-fat Mexican cheese blend
- 1 cup shredded lettuce
- 1 medium tomato, chopped
- ¼ cup minced fresh cilantro

1. In a large skillet, cook beef and onion over medium heat until meat is no longer pink, breaking meat into crumbles; drain. Stir in the salsa, black beans, dressing, taco seasoning and cumin. Place three tortillas in an 11x7-in. baking dish coated with cooking spray. Layer with half of the meat mixture, sour cream and cheese. Repeat layers.

2. Cover and bake at 400° for 25 minutes. Uncover; bake 5-10 minutes longer or until heated through. Let stand for 5 minutes; top with lettuce, tomato and cilantro.

PER SERVING 357 cal., 12 g fat (5 g sat. fat), 45 mg chol., 864 mg sodium, 37 g carb., 3 g fiber, 23 g pro. **Diabetic Exchanges:** 3 lean meat, 2 starch, 1 vegetable, 1 fat.

TOP TIP

Have leftover flour tortillas? Use them to fix a no-fuss dessert for a Mexican meal. Just brush the tortillas with butter, sprinkle on cinnamon-sugar, cut them into wedges and bake on a cookie sheet until crisp.

Comforting Chicken Noodle Casserole

Who knew that a creamy, cheesy noodle casserole could be light? I discovered the recipe for it on a cooking show and made a few changes to better suit our tastes. Everyone requests a big scoop.
—**SYLVIA MCCRONE** DANVILLE, IL

PREP: 20 MIN. • **BAKE:** 40 MIN.
MAKES: 8 SERVINGS

- 5 cups uncooked egg noodles
- 1 cup frozen peas
- 1 celery rib, chopped
- 1 medium carrot, chopped
- 4 cups cubed cooked chicken breast
- 1 can (14¾ ounces) cream-style corn
- 1 can (10¾ ounces) reduced-fat reduced-sodium condensed cream of chicken soup, undiluted
- 2 cups (8 ounces) shredded reduced-fat Colby-Monterey Jack cheese, divided
- 1 small onion, chopped
- ¼ cup chopped green pepper
- ¼ cup chopped sweet red pepper
- ¼ teaspoon pepper

1. In a large saucepan, cook the noodles according to package directions, adding the peas, celery and carrot during the last 5 minutes of cooking. Drain.

2. Stir in chicken, corn, soup, 1 cup cheese, onion, green and red peppers and pepper. Transfer to a 13x9-in. baking dish coated with cooking spray.

3. Cover and bake at 350° for 30 minutes. Sprinkle with the remaining cheese; bake 10 minutes longer or until cheese is melted.

PER SERVING 367 cal., 9 g fat (5 g sat. fat), 92 mg chol., 606 mg sodium, 37 g carb., 3 g fiber, 34 g pro. **Diabetic Exchanges:** 4 lean meat, 2 starch, 1 vegetable.

TOP TIP

Reduced-fat cheese contains at least 25% less fat than the original version and may be used in most recipes that require heating or melting cheese. Fat-free cheese must contain less than 0.5g of fat per serving and is best used in recipes that do not require heating or melting.

Dilled Fish and Vegetable Packet

Perfect for anyone counting calories, this foil-packet dinner is so tasty and quick to fix. I like it best with baked potatoes.
—**SHIRLEY GEVER** TOMS RIVER, NJ

PREP: 15 MIN. • **BAKE:** 20 MIN.
MAKES: 4 SERVINGS

4	tilapia fillets (4 ounces each)
	Refrigerated butter-flavored spray
½	teaspoon salt, divided
¼	teaspoon pepper, divided
2	cups fresh snow peas
2	cups fresh baby carrots, halved lengthwise
1	green onion, thinly sliced
2	tablespoons minced fresh dill
2	garlic cloves, minced
½	cup white wine or reduced-sodium chicken broth

1. Place an 18x12-in. piece of heavy-duty foil on a large baking sheet. Arrange fillets in a single layer on foil; spritz with butter-flavored spray. Sprinkle with ¼ teaspoon salt and ⅛ teaspoon pepper.

2. Combine peas, carrots, onion, dill, garlic and remaining salt and pepper; spoon over the fish. Drizzle with wine. Top with a second large piece of foil. Bring edges of foil pieces together; crimp to seal, forming a large packet. Bake at 400° for 20-25 minutes or until fish flakes easily with a fork and vegetables are crisp-tender. Open the foil carefully to allow steam to escape.

PER SERVING 178 cal., 2 g fat (1 g sat. fat), 55 mg chol., 396 mg sodium, 13 g carb., 4 g fiber, 24 g pro. **Diabetic Exchanges:** 3 lean meat, 2 vegetable.

POTLUCK

Sausage Spinach Pasta Bake

Sometimes I change up this dish by swapping in other meats, such as chicken sausage, veal or ground pork. I've also added mushrooms, summer squash, zucchini and green beans, depending on what's in season. Have fun doing some experimenting of your own!
—**KIM FORNI** LACONIA, NH

PREP: 35 MIN. • **BAKE:** 25 MIN.
MAKES: 10 SERVINGS

1   package (16 ounces) whole wheat spiral pasta
1   pound Italian turkey sausage links, casings removed
1   medium onion, chopped
5   garlic cloves, minced
1   can (28 ounces) crushed tomatoes
1   can (14½ ounces) diced tomatoes, undrained
1   teaspoon dried oregano
1   teaspoon dried basil
¼   teaspoon pepper
1   package (10 ounces) frozen chopped spinach, thawed and squeezed dry
½   cup half-and-half cream
2   cups (8 ounces) shredded part-skim mozzarella cheese
½   cup grated Parmesan cheese

1. Preheat oven to 350°. Cook the pasta according to the package directions.

2. Meanwhile, in a large skillet, cook the turkey sausage and onion over medium heat until the meat is no longer pink. Add garlic. Cook 1 minute longer; drain. Stir in the tomatoes, oregano, basil and pepper. Bring to a boil. Reduce heat; simmer, uncovered, 10 minutes.

3. Drain pasta; stir into sausage mixture. Add spinach and cream; heat through. Transfer to a 13x9-in. baking dish coated with cooking spray. Sprinkle with cheeses. Bake, uncovered, 25-30 minutes or until golden brown.

PER SERVING 377 cal., 11 g fat (5 g sat. fat), 50 mg chol., 622 mg sodium, 45 g carb., 8 g fiber, 25 g pro. **Diabetic Exchanges:** 3 lean meat, 2 starch, 2 vegetable, ½ fat.

TOP TIP

If you wish to grate your own Parmesan instead of using store-bought grated cheese, use the finest section on your grating tool. Or process 1-in. cheese cubes, 1 cup at a time, on high in a food processor or blender until finely grated.

Turkey Wild Rice Casserole

Here's a wonderful home-style turkey meal. The wild rice mixture and tenderloins go in the same baking dish, which makes both serving and cleanup a breeze.
—LOIS KINNEBERG PHOENIX, AZ

PREP: 1 HOUR • **BAKE:** 1 HOUR
MAKES: 6 SERVINGS

- 3 cups water
- 1 cup uncooked wild rice
- 1/2 cup chopped onion
- 1/2 cup chopped carrot
- 1/2 cup chopped celery
- 1 tablespoon butter
- 1 tablespoon canola oil
- 3 tablespoons all-purpose flour
- 1/2 teaspoon rubbed sage
- 1/2 teaspoon salt, divided
- 1/8 teaspoon pepper
- 3/4 cup reduced-sodium chicken broth
- 1/2 cup fat-free milk
- 2 turkey breast tenderloins (3/4 pound each)
- 1 teaspoon dried parsley
- 1/8 teaspoon paprika

1. In a small saucepan, bring the water, wild rice and onion to a boil. Reduce heat; cover and simmer for 55-60 minutes or until rice is tender. Meanwhile, in another saucepan, saute the carrot and celery in butter and oil until tender.

2. Combine the flour, sage, 1/4 teaspoon salt and pepper; stir into carrot mixture until blended. Gradually add the broth and milk. Bring to a boil; cook and stir for 1 minute or until thickened. Remove from the heat. Stir in rice. Transfer to a 2-qt. baking dish coated with cooking spray.

3. Place turkey tenderloins over rice mixture. Combine parsley, paprika and remaining salt; sprinkle over the turkey. Cover and bake at 350° for 60-70 minutes or until a meat thermometer inserted into the turkey reads 170°. Slice turkey; serve with rice.

PER SERVING 313 cal., 5 g fat (2 g sat. fat), 87 mg chol., 371 mg sodium, 29 g carb., 3 g fiber, 36 g pro. **Diabetic Exchanges:** 3 lean meat, 1 1/2 starch, 1 vegetable.

Cheesy Hamburger Noodle Bake, p. 245

CHAPTER 10

COOKING FOR 2

When you're setting a table for two, enjoy downsized dishes.

Saucy Garlic Chicken

I like to assemble this entree ahead of time. Just before dinner, I pop it into the oven and cook the pasta. A sauce of roasted garlic and Parmesan cheese is a rich complement to the chicken and fresh spinach.

—**JOANNA JOHNSON** FLOWER MOUND, TX

PREP: 40 MIN. + COOLING • **BAKE:** 35 MIN.
MAKES: 2 SERVINGS

- 2 whole garlic bulbs
- 1 tablespoon olive oil, divided
- 4½ cups fresh baby spinach
- ½ teaspoon salt, divided
- ¼ teaspoon coarsely ground pepper, divided
- 2 boneless skinless chicken breast halves (6 ounces each)
- 2 tablespoons butter, cubed
- 2 tablespoons all-purpose flour
- 1½ cups 2% milk
- 1¼ cups grated Parmesan cheese, divided
   Dash ground nutmeg
   Hot cooked pasta
   Chopped tomato and minced fresh parsley, optional

1. Remove papery outer skin from garlic (do not peel or separate cloves). Cut tops off of garlic bulbs; brush bulbs with half the oil. Wrap each bulb in heavy-duty foil. Bake at 425° for 30-35 minutes or until softened. Cool for 10-15 minutes.

2. Meanwhile, place spinach in a greased 11x7-in. baking dish; sprinkle with half the salt and pepper. In a large skillet, brown chicken in the remaining oil on both sides; place over spinach.

3. In a large saucepan, melt the butter. Stir in the flour until smooth; gradually add the milk. Bring to a boil; cook and stir for 1-2 minutes or until thickened. Stir in 1 cup cheese, nutmeg and remaining salt. Transfer to a blender; squeeze softened garlic into the blender. Cover and process until smooth. Pour mixture over chicken.

4. Cover; bake at 425° for 30-35 minutes or until a meat thermometer reads 170° and sauce is bubbly. Uncover; sprinkle with remaining cheese. Bake 5 minutes longer. Serve with pasta. Sprinkle with tomato and parsley if desired.

Seafood Thermidor

Here in the Midwest, lobster can be pricey. I discovered a dish that tastes like Lobster Thermidor but uses fish and shrimp instead.

—**SANDI LASKOWSKI** RAPID CITY, SD

START TO FINISH: 25 MIN.
MAKES: 2 SERVINGS

- 2 tablespoons chopped onion
- 2 tablespoons butter, divided
- 3 tablespoons condensed cream of chicken, cream of mushroom or cream of celery soup, undiluted
- 1 teaspoon all-purpose flour
- ¾ cup 2% milk
- 2 tablespoons white wine or chicken broth
- 1 teaspoon lemon juice
- ½ pound cod, haddock or orange roughy fillets, cut into ½-inch cubes
- ¼ pound uncooked medium shrimp, peeled, deveined and cut into thirds
- 2 to 3 tablespoons shredded part-skim mozzarella cheese
- 1 tablespoon minced fresh parsley
- ¼ cup dry bread crumbs
- 1 tablespoon grated Parmesan cheese

1. In a large saucepan, saute the onion in 1 tablespoon butter until tender. Combine the cream soup and flour; stir into onion until blended. Gradually whisk in milk. Stir in the white wine or chicken broth and lemon juice. Bring to a boil; cook and stir for 1-2 minutes or until thickened.

2. Add the cod; cook for 1½ minutes. Stir in the shrimp; cook 1 minute longer or until the fish flakes easily with a fork and the shrimp turn pink. Remove from heat; stir in mozzarella cheese and parsley until cheese is melted.

3. Transfer to a 3-cup baking dish coated with cooking spray. Melt the remaining butter; toss with the bread crumbs and Parmesan cheese. Sprinkle over seafood mixture. Broil 4-6 in. from the heat for 3 minutes or until topping is golden.

TOP TIP

To keep lemon juice handy for recipes, juice some lemons and freeze the juice in ice cube trays. When you need lemon juice, simply defrost the amount you need.

Cordon Bleu Bake

This tasty casserole based on traditional Chicken Cordon Bleu is not only easy to prepare, it's also a great way to use leftovers.
—**HELEN MUSENBROCK** O'FALLON, MO

PREP: 20 MIN. • **BAKE:** 30 MIN.
MAKES: 2 SERVINGS

- ½ cup water
- 3 tablespoons butter, divided
- 1 cup stuffing mix
- 1 cup frozen mixed vegetables, thawed
- ⅔ cup condensed cream of mushroom or cream of chicken soup, undiluted, divided
- ¾ cup cubed cooked chicken breast
- 2 ounces thinly sliced lean deli ham, cut into strips
- ½ cup shredded Swiss cheese

1. In a small saucepan, bring the water and 1 tablespoon butter to a boil. Stir in stuffing mix. Remove from the heat; cover and let stand for 5 minutes.

2. Meanwhile, in a shallow 1-qt. baking dish coated with cooking spray, combine the vegetables with ⅓ cup soup. Combine the chicken with remaining soup; spoon over vegetables. Layer with ham and cheese. Fluff stuffing with a fork; spoon over cheese. Melt remaining butter; drizzle over stuffing. Bake, uncovered, at 350° for 30-35 minutes or until heated through.

Taco Ramekins

I love to cook and eat just about every type of food. This yummy taco bake is one of my favorite dishes—but I think its biggest fans are my daughter and her friends. They like the Mexican-style ingredients that have plenty of zip yet aren't too spicy.
—**BARBARA WILLMITCH** YOUNGSTOWN, OH

PREP: 15 MIN. • **BAKE:** 20 MIN.
MAKES: 2 SERVINGS

- ¼ pound lean ground beef (90% lean)
- ¼ teaspoon chili powder
- ⅛ teaspoon salt
- ⅛ teaspoon pepper
- ¾ cup biscuit/baking mix
- 3 tablespoons cold water
- 1 medium tomato, sliced
- ¼ cup chopped green pepper
- 2 tablespoons sour cream
- 2 tablespoons mayonnaise
- 2 tablespoons shredded cheddar cheese
- 1 tablespoon chopped onion

1. In a skillet, cook the beef over medium heat until no longer pink, breaking into crumbles; drain. Stir in chili powder, salt and pepper. Remove from heat; set aside.

2. Combine biscuit mix and water to form a soft dough. Press onto the bottom and up the sides of two 10-oz. ramekins or custard cups coated with cooking spray. Fill with meat mixture; top with tomato and green pepper. Combine the sour cream, mayonnaise, cheese and onion; spread evenly over the tops.

3. Bake, uncovered, at 375° for 20-25 minutes or until heated through.

DID YOU KNOW?

The best way to cut through the skin of a tomato is with a serrated, not straight-edged, knife. Cut a tomato vertically, from stem end to blossom end, for slices that will be less juicy and hold their shape better.

Portobello Spaghetti Casserole

Want to eat meatless? You can't go wrong with this zesty baked spaghetti loaded with satisfying portobello mushrooms and two kinds of cheese. If you prefer, use shiitakes or plain button mushrooms instead.

—MARY SHIVERS ADA, OK

PREP: 30 MIN. • **BAKE:** 40 MIN.
MAKES: 3 SERVINGS

- 4 ounces uncooked spaghetti
- 3 portobello mushrooms, stems removed and thinly sliced
- ¼ teaspoon salt
- ⅛ teaspoon pepper
- 1 tablespoon olive oil
- 1 egg
- ¼ cup sour cream
- 2 tablespoons grated Parmesan cheese
- 1 tablespoon minced fresh parsley
- 1½ teaspoons all-purpose flour
- ¼ teaspoon garlic powder
- ⅛ teaspoon crushed red pepper flakes
- 1¼ cups marinara sauce
- ¾ cup shredded part-skim mozzarella cheese

1. Cook the spaghetti according to the package directions. Meanwhile, in a large skillet, saute the portobello mushrooms, salt and pepper in oil until mushrooms are tender; drain.

2. In a large bowl, combine the egg, sour cream, Parmesan cheese, parsley, flour, garlic powder and pepper flakes. Drain spaghetti; add to sour cream mixture.

3. Transfer to a 1½-qt. baking dish coated with cooking spray. Top with mushrooms and marinara sauce.

4. Cover and bake at 350° for 30 minutes. Uncover; sprinkle with the mozzarella cheese. Bake 10-15 minutes longer or until a meat thermometer reads 160° and cheese is melted. Let stand 10 minutes before serving.

Italian Sausage Rice Casserole

You'll need just 10 minutes to get this easy dish into the oven. Half an hour of baking leaves plenty of time to toss together a green salad. And just like that, dinner's done!
—**ELEANOR DEAVER** FRESNO, CA

PREP: 10 MIN. • **BAKE:** 30 MIN.
MAKES: 2 SERVINGS

½   pound bulk Italian sausage
¼   cup chopped onion
¼   cup chopped sweet red pepper
½   cup uncooked instant rice
¼   teaspoon dried basil
1   can (10¾ ounces) condensed tomato soup, undiluted
¼   cup water
¼   cup plus 2 tablespoons shredded part-skim mozzarella cheese, divided

1. In a small skillet, cook the Italian sausage, onion and pepper over medium heat until the sausage is no longer pink, breaking sausage into crumbles; drain. Remove from the heat. Stir in rice, basil, tomato soup, water and ¼ cup mozzarella cheese.

2. Transfer to an ungreased 3-cup baking dish. Cover and bake at 350° for 25-30 minutes or until the rice is tender. Uncover; sprinkle with remaining cheese. Bake 5 minutes longer or until cheese is melted.

Tempting Turkey Casserole

Have just a small amount of turkey left over from the holidays? Instead of tossing it out, cube the meat and enjoy it the next night in a fuss-free casserole. It's the perfect dinner when you get back from the traditional day-after-Thanksgiving shopping spree.

—DONNA EVANS MAYVILLE, WI

PREP: 15 MIN. • **BAKE:** 25 MIN.
MAKES: 3 SERVINGS

- 3 ounces uncooked spaghetti, broken into 2-inch pieces
- 1/2 cup process cheese sauce, warmed
- 1/4 cup 2% milk
- 1 1/2 cups frozen chopped broccoli, thawed
- 3/4 cup cubed cooked turkey
- 1/3 cup canned mushroom stems and pieces, drained
- 1 tablespoon pimientos, chopped
- 1/8 to 1/4 teaspoon onion powder
- 1/8 teaspoon poultry seasoning

1. Cook the spaghetti according to the package directions. Meanwhile, in a small bowl, whisk the cheese sauce and milk. Add the broccoli, turkey, mushrooms, pimientos, onion powder and poultry seasoning. Drain the spaghetti; add to broccoli mixture.

2. Transfer to a 1-qt. baking dish coated with cooking spray. Cover; bake at 350° for 25-30 minutes or until heated through.

TOP TIP

To make it easier to measure the correct amounts of ingredients for small-yield recipes, consider buying a countertop food scale that is accurate to the ounce. A scale is a helpful tool when a recipe doesn't call for the entire package of food, such as pasta.

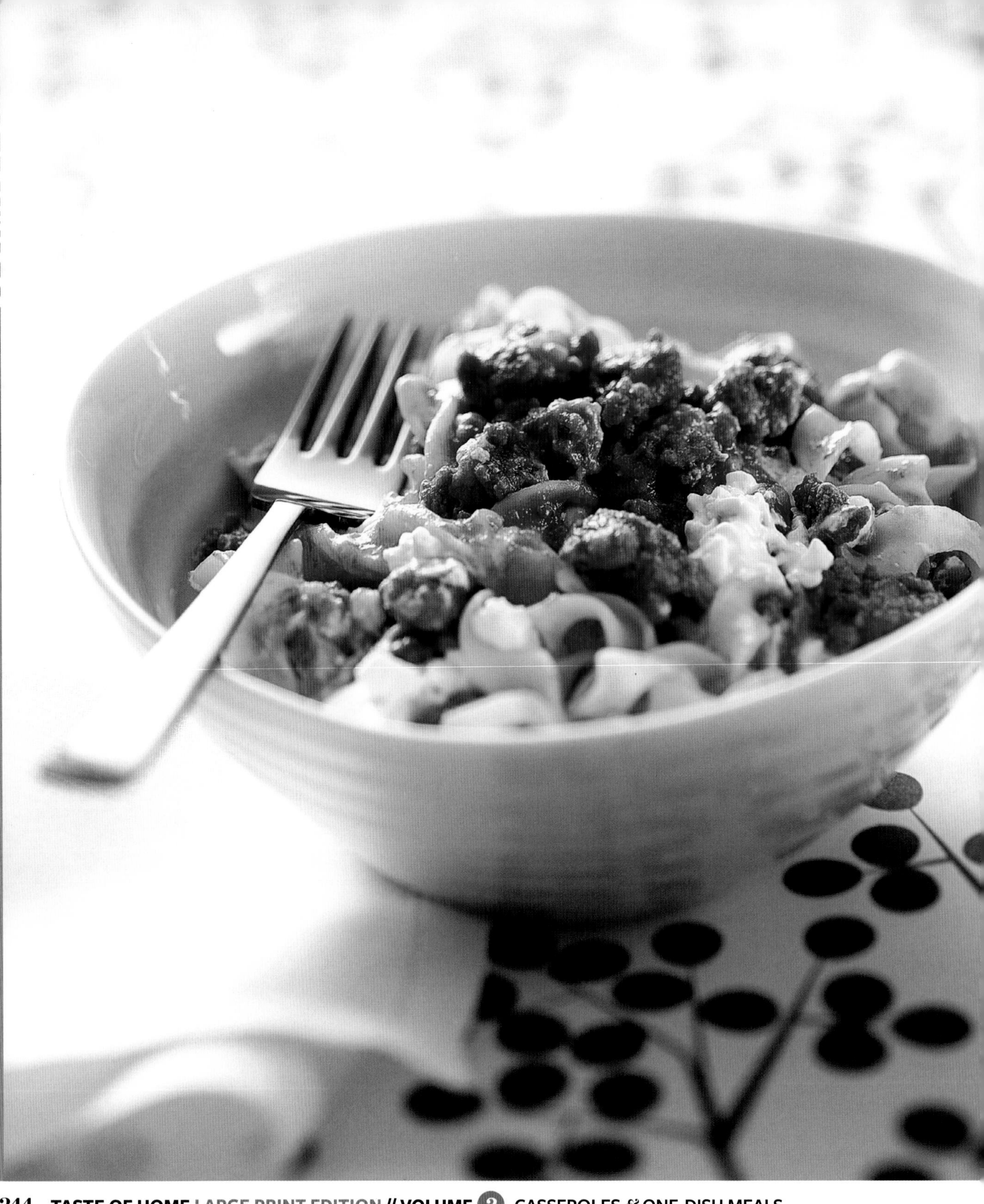

Cheesy Hamburger Noodle Bake

This is no ordinary hamburger casserole! Sour cream and three kinds of cheese add richness to saucy ground beef and noodles.
—**CHARISSA DUNN** BARTLESVILLE, OK

PREP: 35 MIN. • **BAKE:** 20 MIN.
MAKES: 2 SERVINGS

- 2 cups uncooked egg noodles
- 1/2 pound lean ground beef (90% lean)
- 2 tablespoons finely chopped onion
- 1 can (8 ounces) tomato sauce
- 1/4 teaspoon sugar
- 1/8 teaspoon salt
- 1/8 teaspoon garlic salt
  Dash pepper
- 1/4 cup cream-style cottage cheese
- 2 ounces cream cheese, softened
- 1 tablespoon thinly sliced green onion
- 1 tablespoon chopped green pepper
- 1 tablespoon sour cream
- 2 tablespoons grated Parmesan cheese

1. Preheat oven to 350°. Cook the egg noodles according to package directions.

2. Meanwhile, in a large skillet, cook the beef and onion until the meat is no longer pink, breaking meat into crumbles; drain. Remove from heat; stir in tomato sauce, sugar, salt, garlic salt and pepper.

3. In a small bowl, combine the cottage cheese, cream cheese, green onion, green pepper and sour cream.

4. Drain noodles; place half of noodles in a greased 1-qt. baking dish. Spoon half of the beef mixture over the top. Layer with the cottage cheese mixture and remaining noodles. Top with remaining beef mixture; sprinkle with Parmesan cheese.

5. Cover and bake 20-25 minutes or until heated through.

Corn Bread Pork Casserole

A creamy mushroom sauce and corn bread stuffing make ordinary pork chops extra special. It's easy to double or triple the recipe when you have company.

—LADONNA REED PONCA CITY, OK

PREP: 15 MIN. • **BAKE:** 35 MIN.
MAKES: 2 SERVINGS

- 2 boneless pork loin chops (4 ounces each)
- 1/2 pound sliced fresh mushrooms
- 2 tablespoons all-purpose flour
- 1/2 cup reduced-sodium chicken broth
- 1/2 cup reduced-fat sour cream
- 1 tablespoon shredded Parmesan cheese
- 2 garlic cloves, minced
  Pepper to taste
- 1/2 cup crushed corn bread stuffing

1. In a large skillet coated with cooking spray, brown the pork chops on both sides; set aside. In the same skillet, saute the mushrooms until tender. Transfer mushrooms to a 1 1/2-qt. baking dish coated with cooking spray.

2. In a small bowl, combine the flour and chicken broth until smooth. Stir in the sour cream, Parmesan cheese, garlic and pepper; pour over the mushrooms. Top with pork chops.

3. Cover and bake at 350° for 25 minutes. Sprinkle with the corn bread stuffing. Bake 10 minutes longer or until a meat thermometer reads 160°.

Ham and Noodle Bake

I hit on this recipe when I had extra deli ham in the fridge. Now I'm always happy when I have leftovers because I can enjoy this!
—**LAURA BURGESS** MOUNT VERNON, SD

PREP: 25 MIN. • **BAKE:** 30 MIN.
MAKES: 3 SERVINGS

- 2 cups uncooked egg noodles
- 1 cup cubed deli ham
- 1/2 cup shredded cheddar cheese
- 1/2 cup condensed cream of celery soup, undiluted
- 1/3 cup 2% milk
- 1 teaspoon finely chopped onion
- 2 teaspoons butter, melted, divided
- 1/4 teaspoon poppy seeds
- 1/4 teaspoon dried oregano
- 1/8 teaspoon salt
- 1/8 teaspoon dried basil
- 3 tablespoons dry bread crumbs

1. Cook the egg noodles according to the package directions. Meanwhile, in a small bowl, combine the deli ham, cheese, soup, milk, onion, 1 teaspoon butter, poppy seeds and seasonings. Drain the noodles; add to ham mixture.

2. Transfer to a 1 1/2-qt. baking dish coated with cooking spray. Combine the crumbs and remaining butter; sprinkle over the casserole. Bake, uncovered, at 325° for 30-35 minutes or until heated through.

TOP TIP

If you usually cook for two and often can't use up the vegetables you buy before they go bad, consider buying them from the supermarket salad bar. You can get the small amounts you need for recipes and won't be spending money on food that will eventually be thrown away.

GENERAL RECIPE INDEX

ALPHABETICAL RECIPE INDEX